MICHIGAN FREE

MICHIGAN FREE

Your Comprehensive Guide
to FREE Travel, Recreation, &
Entertainment Opportunities

ERIC FREEDMAN

Ann Arbor
THE UNIVERSITY OF MICHIGAN PRESS

Copyright © by the University of Michigan 1993
All rights reserved
ISBN 0-472-08200-0
Published in the United States of America by
The University of Michigan Press
Manufactured in the United States of America

1996 1995 1994 1993   4 3 2 1

Paperback ISBN: 978-0-472-08200-1

To Mary Ann, Ian, and Cara,
who explore Michigan's treasures with me

Contents

Welcome to Michigan, the Free Way   1

Outdoors in Michigan

  1. National Parks   5
     Free View: Pictured Rocks National Lakeshore, Grand Marais

  2. Nature Preserves   16
     Free View: Five Lakes Muskegon Nature Sanctuary, Muskegon

  3. National Wildlife Refuges   28

  4. Nature Centers   33

  5. National Forests   42
     Free View: MacKenzie Ski Trails, Cadillac

  6. Outdoor Opportunities   49

  7. Fishing   56

Culture and Entertainment

  8. Museums   65
     Free View: Michigan Iron Industry Museum, Negaunee

  9. Orchestra, Theater, and Dance Performances   101

Touring

  10. Wineries   109
     Free View: Lemon Creek Winery, Berrien Springs

  11. Colleges and Universities   117

CONTENTS

12.	Industry and Business	138
13.	Government Attractions Free View: State Capitol, Lansing	147
14.	Walking Tours Free View: Grand Ledge Historic District, Grand Ledge	152
15.	Scenic Drives	162
16.	Cemeteries Free View: U.S. Post Cemetery, Mackinac Island	165

More to Do

17.	Ideas for Children Free View: Belle Isle Aquarium, Detroit	171
18.	A Potpourri for Adults and Families Free View: Mackinac Bridge Walk, St. Ignace	180
19.	Festivals Free View: Tulip Time Festival, Holland	192
20.	Tips for Free Way Travelers	202
21.	Low-Cost Lodging	205
	Appendix: Travel and Recreation Information Sources	211
	Index	241

Welcome to Michigan, the Free Way

Everything costs more these days, or so it seems.

Gas is up. So are motel rooms, restaurant meals, tolls, and camping fees. "Service" stations don't provide service, and many even charge for air.

But don't let that economic reality become an excuse to bury hopes of a long-distance vacation, a weekend adventure, or a series of day trips in Michigan.

The truth—kept secret for too long—is that some things *don't* cost more these days: they were free before, and they're still free. There are enough free things to experience, see, savor, participate in, and enjoy to fill your scrapbooks and your memories. It doesn't matter whether you like indoor activities or prefer the out-of-doors, whether you live in Michigan or just plan to visit, or whether you travel with children or not. There's plenty to do without spending a lot of money to do it.

Michigan Free tells you how to find free concerts, plays, museums, and guided tours. There's detailed information about national parks and forests, fish hatcheries, college campus activities, live theater and dance, concerts and government buildings, wineries and factories, nature centers and festivals, cemeteries, walking tours, and more.

This is an *independent* guide. That means there are no ads, and no business, organization, government agency, or attraction paid to be included. It's as up to date as possible, although admission policies and hours can and do change. Your comments and suggestions are welcome.

Enjoy Michigan, the free way.

Outdoors in Michigan

Chapter 1

National Parks

Three national parks, all on the Great Lakes and all without an admission fee, are located in Michigan. Each park offers spectacular scenery, natural history, and recreational opportunities.

NORTHWEST

Sleeping Bear Dunes National Lakeshore

Superintendent (616) 326-5134
Sleeping Bear Dunes National Lakeshore Open year-round
Box 277
Empire MI 49630

History. According to Chippewa legend, a forest fire in Wisconsin drove a mother bear and her two cubs across Lake Michigan to the Leelanau Peninsula. Although the mother swam safely to the Michigan shore, both cubs drowned within view of the coast. Years later, a massive sand dune above the shore marks the place where the mother bear waited helplessly and futilely for her young to arrive; it was there that grief killed her. Two islands, 5,300-acre South Manitou and 15,000-acre North Manitou, now mark the final resting places of the doomed cubs.

Not surprisingly, geologists offer a different account, noting that this area was scoured by glaciers during the Ice Age. The beach dunes were formed from beach sand, scientists say, and the higher, perched dunes were made by glacial sand.

Congress established Sleeping Bear Dunes National Lakeshore in 1970. The park's 70,000 acres now include both Manitou islands and part of the mainland in Benzie and Leelanau counties.

Free Activities and Attractions
- The Philip A. Hart Visitor Center is open daily, year-round, with history and nature exhibits and a slide show. It's three miles north of Empire on M-109.
- Rangers lead guided walks and evening programs in the summer.
- The Dune Climb, north of the visitor center, is the most popular attraction in the park, especially among children and energetic adults. Those who reach the crest 130 feet above the base earn a view of Glen Lake.
- Hiking and cross-country ski trails pass along the dunes, forests, and meadows. Trail maps are available at the visitor center.
- The 7.1-mile Pierce Stocking Scenic Drive overlooks the dunes, Glen Lake, and Lake Michigan, with 12 designated stopping places along the route. A free, self-guiding brochure describes the human and natural history at each overlook. The drive is open from mid-May through early November, weather permitting.

Sleeping Bear Dunes National Lakeshore. (Courtesy Michigan Travel Bureau.)

- In the village on South Manitou, there is a visitor center in the old post office, with exhibits about the island's natural and human history. It's open daily from mid-June until Labor Day and on weekends through September. Visitors also can see the island's 1871 lighthouse (the light has been out of service since 1958); Valley of the Giants, an impressive grove of virgin white cedars; a gull colony; abandoned farmsteads; and more sand dunes.
- Canoeing and kayaking are allowed on the creeks and rivers that pass through the park.
- The Sleeping Bear Point Coast Guard Station Maritime Museum is located near the Dune Climb and D. H. Day Campground. It highlights the history of the U.S. Lifesaving Service and U.S. Lighthouse Service, predecessors of today's Coast Guard (for more information, see chap. 8).
- Wilderness camping with a free permit is allowed on both islands and the mainland.
- Boat launches are located along the Lake Michigan shore and inland streams and lakes. North Manitou Island lacks protected anchorage; boats can use the island's docks for up to 15 minutes only to load and unload but must moor offshore. South Manitou Island has no public docking.
- Fishing for salmon, bass, trout, and pike is popular. A state license is required.
- Swimming is allowed in Lake Michigan and inland waters.
- Manitou Passage Bottomland Preserve lies off the park shore. Despite the presence of lighthouses on South Manitou since 1840, many ships have run aground or sunk here. The preserve is highly regarded for its shallow water scuba diving opportunities, and constantly shifting sands alternatively expose and cover wrecks and reefs. Among them are the steamer *Francisco Morazan*, wrecked in shallow waters in 1960; the schooner *Josephine Dresden*, sunk alongside a dock on North Manitou in 1907; and the schooner *Supply*, lost in an 1862 storm.

Fees. Established campgrounds on the mainland and South Manitou Island; ferry service to the islands; canoe rentals.

Location. The park is 25 miles west of Traverse City. Route M-22 runs through the park. Both Manitou islands are accessible by private boat, ferry, and licensed chartered boat.

UPPER PENINSULA

Isle Royale National Park

Superintendent
Isle Royale National Park
Houghton MI 49931

(906) 482-0984
Open from mid-May through mid-October

History. For a thousand years, native Americans paddled to Isle Royale in the northwestern part of Lake Superior to obtain copper. In the 1830s, commercial fishing began on the 210-square-mile island, followed by settlers and farmers. By the late 1800s, commercial copper mines operated with little economic success, but the island became popular as a summer vacation and excursion spot. In 1940, Congress established it as a national park, with a wilderness emphasis; it was later designated as a United Nations biosphere reserve. It's internationally renowned for its wolf and moose populations.

Free Activities and Attractions
- Visitors can take their canoes and kayaks on the ferry from the mainland for use on the island's bays and inland lakes, although landing spots on the outer shore of Lake Superior are scarce, and weather can turn windy or stormy with little advance notice. Designated canoe routes are on the northeast half of the island; 16 portages, ranging from 0.1 mile to 2.0 miles in length, are marked with a white *P* on posts.
- Fishing in Lake Superior requires a Michigan license, but no license is necessary for inland streams and lakes. Lake, brook, and rainbow trout, northern pike, walleye, and yellow perch are the most sought-after species.
- Hiking trails extend for 166 miles, and it generally takes about five days to cover the 45-mile length of the island between Windigo and Rock Harbor. Visitors are cautioned against cross-country, off-trail hiking due to swamps, bogs, and dense vegetation.
- Swimming is not recommended because of the extremely cold water in Lake Superior and leeches in the warmer, inland lakes.
- The chilly waters around Lake Superior are the graveyard for at least 10 major wrecks and dozens of their crew members, and divers also are attracted to underwater copper veins. Collecting greenstones is allowed. Divers must obtain a free permit at a ranger station. Accessible

wrecks include the steamer *Algona,* run aground in 1885; the freighter *America,* sunk in 1928; the sidewheeler *Cumberland,* lost in 1877; the freighter *Emperor,* wrecked in 1947; and the freighter *Chester A. Congdon,* run aground and broken up in a 1918 storm.
- Camping is on a first-come first-served basis, with a free permit. Some sites are accessible only by kayak or canoe.

Fees. Canoe rentals; ferry service; lodging at Rock Harbor.

Location. The park, an archipelago, is linked to the mainland by ferries from Houghton, Michigan (73 miles, 6 hours) and Copper Harbor, Michigan (56 miles, 4 1/2 hours), and from Grand Portage, Minnesota (22 miles, 3 hours). There's an extra charge for canoes, kayaks, motor boats, motors, and air tanks. You can also reach the park by float plane or private boat. No motorized vehicles are allowed on the island.

Isle Royale National Park. (Courtesy Michigan Travel Bureau.)

Pictured Rocks National Lakeshore

Superintendent (906) 387-2607
Pictured Rocks National Lakeshore Open year-round
Box 40
Munising MI 49862

History. Site of the first national lakeshore, the pastel-colored cliffs of Pictured Rocks were long known to the Ojibway, who fished and hunted here and traveled through en route to their summer fishing grounds off the St. Marys River to the east. French missionaries, trappers, and explorers reached the area in the 1600s, followed in the early nineteenth century by settlers lured by the white pine forests. The park, long and narrow, is more than 60,000 acres in size.

Free Activities and Attractions
- The Munising Information Center, operated jointly by the National Park Service and U.S. Forest Service, is open all year. Exhibits provide an orientation to recreational opportunities at both Pictured Rocks and Hiawatha National Forest.
- The Munising Falls Interpretive Center is open only in the summer. Its exhibits focus on the history of blast furnaces, logging and forestry in the area, as well as local geology. A short walk takes visitors behind the free-flowing waters of Munising Falls.
- The Grand Sable Visitor Center is open only in the summer. Here, between Lake Superior and Grand Sable Lake, are four square miles of wind-deposited sand dunes. The center provides a general orientation to the park and an exhibit about dune formation.
- Small boats and canoes are permitted on Grand Sable Lake, which has a boat launch, and on Beaver Lake and Little Beaver Lake, which don't. Canoeing on the park's rivers and streams is hampered by brush and shallowness. There are public launches at Munising and Grand Marais with access to Lake Superior.
- Fishing with a state license is allowed on Lake Superior, on backcountry ponds and lakes, and on the park's streams and rivers. Ice fishing is popular on Munising Bay and most of the inland lakes.
- The Grand Marais Maritime Museum and ranger station at Coast Guard Point depict the early years of shipping, commercial fishing, lighthouses, the U.S. Life Saving Service, and shipwrecks. The museum is

open daily during the summer and intermittently the rest of the year (for more information, see chap. 8).
- Rangers lead interpretive walks and programs throughout the summer on such subjects as shipwrecks and lighthouses, cultural history of the area, glacial history, geology, and Ojibway crafts. There also are fireside chats during the spring and fall.
- The Au Sable Light Station, which began operating at Au Sable Point in 1874, is a 1.5-mile walk from the Hurricane River campground in the northeast part of the park. This well-preserved lighthouse is listed on the National Register of Historic Places. It's open to summer visitors three times a week during ranger-led programs.
- Camping is allowed at designated backcountry sites, with a free permit.
- Hiking can take the form of either short walks from parking areas to natural formations or overnight and multiday hikes along the trails. The North Country National Scenic Trail between New York and North Dakota passes through the park for 42.8 miles.
- There are four nature trails with numbered posts and interpretive brochures. The White Pine Trail, Sand Point March Trail, and Miners Fall Trail are each less than a mile long. The White Birch Trail is two miles long. The marked locations highlight the area's natural and human histories.
- Marked cross-country ski trails, many of which are groomed, and snowmobile trails extend throughout the park. Snowshoeing is also popular.
- The Alger Bottomland Preserve is located off the park shore, with shipwrecks, colorful underwater rocks and cliffs, and weedbeds for fish. Wrecks here include the steamer *Herman H. Hettler*, which struck a reef during a 1926 gale; the steamer *Manhattan*, which burned and sank after the crew lost control in 1903; and the sidewheeler *Superior*, which ran aground against the cliffs in 1856.

Fees. Campgrounds.

Location. The national park is accessible by motor vehicle from Grand Marais to the east and from Munising to the west.

FREE VIEW: PICTURED ROCKS NATIONAL LAKESHORE, GRAND MARAIS

Most visitors claim the formation named Chapel Rock resembles a mystical castle or church. But from my vantage point atop a cliff to the west, it looks malevolent rather than regal or religious, a giant multihued skull with gaping eyeholes that stare relentlessly over Lake Superior. Its horrendous grin gloats over the graveyard of many Great Lakes vessels.

Nature will have revenge, however. Just as thousands of years of natural forces shaped the sandstone into this thing of wonder, the power of weather, waves, and wind continue to nibble and gouge away at Chapel Rock, returning it, piece by piece, to sand.

This is Pictured Rocks National Lakeshore, stretching along the northern shore of the Upper Peninsula between Grand Marais and Munising.

Officially the first of America's national lakeshores, this was familiar territory to the Chippewa. French explorers and Jesuit missionaries passed these startling cliffs and sand dunes in search of wealth, territory, and souls. Father Jacques Marquette, the best known of the region's early priests, reputedly preached to the Indians from Miners Castle, another large formation. Today's visitor can feel, as the Indians did, that spirits are present in these stones of many colors.

Although the distance from end to end is relatively short and the park itself is never more than three miles wide, the terrain varies tremendously. There are sand dunes and beaches, high cliffs and waterfalls, lakes and rivers.

With its pounding surf, white sand, driftwood, and gulls pecking for morsels along the beach or soaring above the waves, this could be Cape Cod or the Jersey Shore or Florida's Gulf Coast. Unlike those spots, Lake Superior is shiveringly cold even in the heat of the summer, although our children, seemingly immune to water temperatures that send adults scurrying for towels, enjoyed the waves. The beaches are fertile hunting grounds for brightly colored rocks and pebbles, including agates, smoothed by glacial and water action.

The park's very remoteness makes it a place where imagination can rule, where the juncture of ancient rock and powerful water is far removed from the RV parades and crowded tours of so many other national parks. In fact, it's impossible to see most of the spectacular scenery by car from the one county road—partly unpaved—that gives access to the park. Only one large formation—Miners Castle—the beach at Grand

NATIONAL PARKS

Sable Lake, and a section of glistening Twelvemile Beach are accessible by road.

One of the best ways to see and appreciate Pictured Rocks is by foot. That means hiking, either day walks from trailhead parking lots to the beaches and cliffs or treks with overnight camping along part or all the 43-mile Lakeshore Trail that hugs the coast.

The trail, part of the 3,200-mile North Country National Scenic Trail between New York and North Dakota, has its rough spots. Expect some steep climbs and descents, with roots and stone outcroppings as steps, as well as mud, sand, and low-hanging branches. At other points you'll find wooden boardwalks and log bridges to cross rivers and wetlands.

Leisurely hikes of up to a few miles each begin at various parking areas and end at some of the park's well-known attractions, including Grand Sable Dunes, Miner's Falls, and the Log Slide. At the eastern edge of the park, trails along the dunes—sometimes indistinct in the shifting sands—lead through tough beach grass, goldenrod, and small patches of conifers fighting, with varying degrees of success, for a foothold and survival. From the windswept ridges, you can enjoy the view of Lake Superior's many shades of blue.

Miners Castle, Pictured Rocks National Lakeshore. (Courtesy Michigan Travel Bureau.)

For those who opt to backpack, the park offers a series of free backcountry campgrounds, each with 3 to 15 relatively private sites along the trail. Reservations are allowed, and permits can be picked up from rangers or at the visitor centers. Because these campgrounds are close to the water, sunsets are spectacular when the skies are clear.

There also are three drive-in campgrounds operated by the National Park Service and a fourth run by the Michigan Department of Natural Resources. These, however, do not accept reservations. They charge a fee and fill quickly during vacation season.

Bring binoculars. Don't ignore the frequent overlooks along the trail, vantage points for photographs, rest, and appreciating the setting. In August you can forage for ripe wild blueberries, small and sweet, as we did.

Conifers, beech, sugar maples, birch, and an occasional mountain ash, its reddish orange berries adding brightness to the green foliage, grow along the top of the cliffs. The trail brings you close to several gull rookeries, where you can watch the birds dive for fish.

The cliff walls are like natural canvas worked by unknown artists in black, red, orange, white, and gray. Minerals leaching from between the layers of sandstone "paint" the "pictures" that give the park its name. Some resemble the work of modernists, possibly intoxicated, with bright splashes of color, slap-dashedly applied. Other sections look more deliberately designed. My son insisted that one set of black patterns was a cartoon-style horse and rider. Who's to say he's wrong?

Isolated though it may seem, the human presence is visible on the lake, at least temporarily, much like footprints in the sand before they are erased by the rising tide. One evening after supper, perched on a cliff top near our backcountry campsite, we watched a tugboat slowly, so slowly, tow two heavily loaded barges westward. In the morning with the water calm, a small, brightly colored sailboat frolicked along the base of the cliffs, past caves and arches carved into the colored rock by the water. Hiking, we waved to passengers on the tour boats far below us. They, in turn, snapped photos of us backpackers on the trail high above.

That human presence has not always been so transient. After the French and then the British lost control in the late eighteenth century, American settlers began to use and exploit the resources.

This once was timber country, for example, and its white pine helped build the cities of the Midwest. Evidence is still visible at spots such as Kingston Lake, a state forest campground in the national lakeshore's inland buffer zone. Even now, a hike along the Fox River Trail, which leads south from the campground to the Seney National Wildlife Refuge 27.5 miles away, reveals slowly rotting stumps, lasting legacies of the lumbering era.

At the Log Slide inside the park, lumberers shoved logs down a 500-foot wooden chute into Lake Superior for towing to the sawmills. Sand was used to put out the flames when the heat of the friction set the slide ablaze. The slide itself is long gone.

Exploitation also came in the form of charcoal kilns and blast furnaces, fueled by the area's abundant forests, that were used to refine the iron ore mined in the western Upper Peninsula. Artifacts and exhibits about the boom and decline of those endeavors are displayed at the park's Munising Falls Visitor Center, while the forest, in its own quiet but relentless way, has reclaimed the physical ruins of blast furnace operations.

Offshore from the park lies the state's Alger Underwater Preserve, a popular spot for divers who enjoy exploring sunken wrecks, rock formations, and caves. A number of local charter and diving companies offer equipment rentals and tours. Mapped dive sites include the resting places of such nineteenth-century vessels as the steam barge *Smith Moore* and the sidewheel steamer *Superior*. Among the twentieth-century wrecks are the freighter *Manhattan* and the steamer *Kiowa*.

From below at water level, Chapel Rock remains a giant skull vigilantly guarding its realm. I don't argue with those visitors who called it a castle or a church, however, for we all are entitled to our own myths at Pictured Rocks.

Chapter 2

Nature Preserves

A number of nonprofit environmental groups and government agencies operate nature preserves and sanctuaries dedicated to safeguarding habitat, wildlife, and natural features from development, encroachment, and exploitation. Scattered from suburban Detroit to the remote corners of the state, they're open to the public for such gentle uses as hiking, birdwatching, environmental study, photography, snowshoeing, or cross-country skiing. Some preserves have marked nature or hiking trails, but many do not, so it's wise to carry a compass. In some instances, visitors must walk along trails to reach the preserve from a parking lot or the closest road. These preserves were selected as a representative sample from among more than 200 in Michigan.

For detailed directions on how to reach the preserves and information about access restrictions, contact the owners or operators.

Little Traverse Conservancy (616) 347-0991
3264 Powell Road
Harbor Springs MI 49740

Manistee National Forest (616) 775-2421
421 S. Mitchell St. (800) 821-6263
Cadillac MI 49601

Michigan Audubon Society (517) 886-9144
6011 West St. Joseph Highway
Box 80527
Lansing MI 48908-0527

Michigan Department of (517) 373-1220
   Natural Resources
Box 30028
Lansing MI 48909

Michigan Nature Association (313) 324-2626
7981 Beard Road
Box 102
Avoca MI 48006

Montcalm Soil Conservation (517) 831-4606
   District
806 N. State
Stanton MI 48888

Nature Conservancy (517) 332-1741
2840 E. Grand River Drive, Suite 5
East Lansing MI 48823

Many of these groups also maintain other preserves and sanctuaries, some of which may be remote or accessible only with difficulty. To use them, prospective visitors are asked to explore only with a guide from the organization.

SOUTHEAST

Jackson County

Haehnle Sanctuary (887 acres) northeast of Jackson via Seymour Road, Leoni Township. Sandhill cranes nest here, with 2,000 or more seen in late October and early November before migrating to northern Florida. Habitat includes marsh, swamp, hardwood forests, abandoned fields, and wildlife food plots. Michigan Audubon Society.

Kate Palmer Bird Sanctuary (53 acres) west of Jackson via O'Brien Road, Spring Arbor Township. The sanctuary abounds with woodpeckers, flycatchers, warblers, and other birds. There are natural springs, marshland, deciduous woods, and mounds of slate showing where early settlers mined winter coal. Michigan Audubon Society.

Lapeer County

Jonathon Woods Preserve (144 acres) north of Lake Orion via Jonathon Road, Dryden Township. Hills, valleys, and kettleholes create microclimatic differences that support more than 330 plant species plus small mammals and birds. A bog and grove of hemlocks grow in a sheltered ravine. Nature Conservancy.

Monroe County

Erie Marsh Preserve (2,168 acres) southwest of Monroe via Dean Road, Erie Township. A shallow portion of North Maumee Bay covers about half the preserve. The rest is a mosaic of aquatic plants and open water behind a dike system. The area is a migratory and nesting area for waterfowl and shore birds, with great blue herons and great egrets feeding here. Nature Conservancy.

Oakland County

Timberland Swamp Nature Sanctuary (245 acres) west of Clarkston via Ware Road, Springfield Township. Totally surrounded by Huron-Clinton Indian Springs Park, the preserve is a remnant of swampland featuring cathedral-like forest groves, rare flowering shrubs and plants, tens of thousands of trilliums, and a rich summer resident bird population. Michigan Nature Association.

Washtenaw County

Sharon Hollow Preserve (238 acres) northwest of Manchester via Easudes Road, Manchester Township. Botanically rich, the preserve along the River Raisin includes swamps, beach-maple forest, and streams at the edge of a glacial moraine. There is also nearly a mile of pond frontage at the site of an 1834 muley sawmill, now a wine-tasting shop. Nature Conservancy.

SOUTHWEST

Allegan County

Fennville Farm (1,300 acres) south of Fennville via 118th Avenue, Clyde Township. The refuge, part of the Allegan State Game Area, is a waterfowl management area with as many as 25,000 Canada geese at a time during the fall migration season. It also attracts bald and golden eagles, ducks, snow and blue geese, and other migratory birds and provides habitat for deer, pheasants, and rabbits. The refuge itself is off-limits, but most of the geese can be viewed from various points along the road, and visitors are allowed in the adjacent game area. Department of Natural Resources.

Calhoun County

Baker Sanctuary (897 acres) north of Marshall via Junction Road or 14 Mile Road, Convis Township. A refuge for nesting sandhill cranes, it contains floodplain forest, cattail marsh, tamarack bog, oak opening, and wet meadow. There is a mile-long Doty Nature Flower Trail boardwalk. Michigan Audubon Society.

Voorhees Sanctuary (40 acres) northwest of Albion via 24 Mile Road, Lee Township. A natural, unpastured woodlot of beech and maples with a profusion of spring wildflowers. Michigan Audubon Society.

Sharon Hollow Preserve. (Courtesy Nature Conservancy.)

Cass County

Dowagiac Woods (220 acres) southwest of Dowagiac via Frost Street or Sink Road, Pokagon Township. Traversed by an unnamed tributary of the Dowagiac River, there are wetlands and marsh, swamp-type forests, and open brushy areas. The preserve is home to dozens of types of nesting birds, trees, and wildflowers, and boasts more than 150 beds of the scarce blue-eyed Mary that blooms in the spring. Michigan Nature Association.

Kalamazoo County

Mildred Harris Sanctuary (40 acres) northwest of Kalamazoo via F Avenue or 8th Street, Alamo Township. Lying on the tongue of the Kalamazoo Moraine, the preserve is half wooded and hilly, half gently rolling fields, with a mature beech-maple forest and plentiful wildflowers. Michigan Audubon Society.

Van Buren County

Hamilton Township Coastal Plain Marsh Nature Sanctuary (79 acres) via 84th Avenue, Hamilton Township. Marshes like those on the Atlantic coast are here, with typical coastal plain plant life. Michigan Nature Association.

Martha Mott Preserve (80 acres) north of Mattawan via 4th Street, Almena Township. The preserve consists of a sand blow, marsh, prairie, and varied wildlife habitats crossed by a small stream. There is a nature trail. Michigan Audubon Society.

Ross Preserve (1,214 acres) south of South Haven via 38th Street, Covert Township. Ancient sand dunes have created a mosaic of botanical communities, including coastal plain marshes that harbor animals and plants ordinarily found on Atlantic coastal marshes. There also are oak, hemlock, and swamp forests. Eight endangered or threatened species are found here. Nature Conservancy.

CENTRAL

Barry County

Warner Sanctuary (100 acres) southwest of Hastings via Hart Road or Erway Road, Rutland Township. The preserve includes five-acre Warner Lake with an unusual floating bog. Endangered plants have been found here. Michigan Audubon Society.

Montcalm County

Comden-Towle Model Forest (40 acres) northeast of Greenville via Kendaville Road, Douglass Township. The forest features 2.7 miles of trails past hardwoods and conifers, a five-acre timber stand improvement demonstration area, wildlife pond, and shelter house. There's also evidence of past logging and farming. Montcalm Soil Conservation District.

NORTHEAST

Cheboygan County

Agnes Andreae Nature Preserve (27 acres) east of Indian River via Riverwoods Road, Koehler Township. The preserve has 2,000 feet of frontage on the lower Pigeon River with a foot bridge to cross the river. Terrain varies from high bluffs to low conifer swampland. There is a large cabin and, unlike most nature preserves, camping is permitted. Little Traverse Conservancy.

Colonial Point Forest Preserve (283 acres) southeast of Pellston via East Indian Point Road, Burt Township. One of the few remaining old-growth forests in Michigan, it includes a towering stand of mature red oaks more than 150 years old. Nature Conservancy, Little Traverse Conservancy, and University of Michigan Biological Station.

Otsego County

Hoobler Preserve (465 acres) east of Vanderbilt via Old Vanderbilt Road, Dover Township. Featured are a dense white cedar swamp and boggy areas, providing habitat for bear, bobcat, osprey, eagles, and deer. It is now part of Pigeon River Country State Forest. Nature Conservancy and Department of Natural Resources.

Presque Isle County

Besser Natural Area (134 acres) northeast of Alpena via Rayburn Highway, Presque Isle Township. Within the Mackinaw State Forest, the area features a scenic Lake Huron shoreline and mature, virgin red and white pines. Also included are remnants of the abandoned lumbering and shipping village of Bell, as well as a hiking trail with interpretative signs. It is one of about 20 wilderness, wild, and natural areas designated under the DNR's Natural Heritage Program. Department of Natural Resources.

Thompson's Harbor (4,765 acres) southeast of Rogers City via U.S. 23, Krakow Township. Now within the Mackinaw State Forest, the preserve features cobble and dune shoreline, conifer swamp, marl beach pools, marsh, and northern fen. The world's largest population of the rare dwarf lake iris is found here, along with other rare plants and the bald eagle. Nature Conservancy and Department of Natural Resources.

NORTHWEST

Antrim County

Grass River Natural Area (1,050 acres) south of Bellaire via Alden Highway, Forest Home, Helena and Custer Townships. This is a complex of wetland habitats with conifer swamps and marshes, bald eagles, and ospreys. The preserve has an interpretive building and hiking trails. Nature Conservancy and Antrim County.

Jordan River (133 acres) north of Mancelona via Graves Crossing Road, Jordan Township. The preserve protects 1.2 miles of the Jordan River, one of Michigan's premier cold water streams and protected by the federal Wild and Scenic River program. White cedar, firm spruce, birch, and aspen grow along the banks. Nature Conservancy and Mackinaw State Forest.

NATURE PRESERVES

Charlevoix County

Charles A. Ranson Nature Preserve (80 acres) east of Charlevoix via Maple Grove Road, Hayes Township. Mature hardwood forest and open meadows provide a panoramic view from the Leelanau Peninsula to Beaver Island. There are a variety of wild mushrooms and abundant wildflowers, plus a nature trail. Little Traverse Conservancy.

Sleepy Hollow Nature Preserve (55 acres) southeast of Charlevoix via Phelps Road, Eveline Township. The densely wooded preserve is dominated by sugar maple, American beech, and black ash. A stream and an old logging road cuts through, and deer, red fox, mink, and other mammals have been spotted here. Little Traverse Conservancy.

Emmet County

Elmer Johnston Nature Preserve (220 acres) west of Pellston via Church Road, Readmond Township. Rolling hardwood forest and meadowland, with deer, fox, and other wildlife, are at this preserve, along with several stone piles that are evidence the land had previously been tilled for farming. There is a panoramic view of Lake Michigan and Beaver Island. Little Traverse Conservancy.

Menonaqua Woods Nature Preserve (100 acres) northeast of Petoskey via Beach Road, Little Traverse Township. Overlooking Little Traverse Bay, this is a dune ecosystem with steep terrain, a dense beech-maple-hemlock forest, and a cedar swamp. Little Traverse Conservancy.

Round Lake Nature Preserve (60 acres) northeast of Petoskey via Powell Road, Little Traverse Township. Hardwoods and conifers predominate at this preserve, which has 1,500 feet of frontage on Round Lake, freshwater clams, abundant spring wildflowers, and trails. This is the head of the inland water route used by Indians to canoe from Little Traverse Bay to Lake Huron. Little Traverse Conservancy.

West Wequetonsing Nature Preserve (14 acres) via Pennsylvania Avenue, city of Harbor Springs. Primarily swampland at the base of a tall, wave-cut cliff, with soggy muck soil, water-tolerant trees, acres of standing water, and abundant wildflowers and marsh-type plants. Little Traverse Conservancy.

Muskegon County

Five Lakes Muskegon Nature Sanctuary (53 acres) via Evanston Road, Egelston Township. Full of grasses, sedges, rushes, and other weedy-looking plants that turn out not to be weeds, the sanctuary has sandy soil and is considered the preserve with the highest number of threatened, endangered, and special concern plant species in the state. Michigan Nature Association.

Newaygo County

Loda Lake Wild Flower Sanctuary (72 acres) via Felch Avenue, Lincoln Township. A combination of bog, high ground, dry areas, and a small lake, this is a sanctuary for native Michigan plants on national forest land. Among them are such protected species as trillium, bird's foot violet, orchids, trailing arbutus, flowering dogwood, Michigan holly, and club mosses. Manistee National Forest.

UPPER PENINSULA

Alger County

Twin Waterfalls Nature Preserve (15 acres) via H58, city of Munising. Located near the waterfall-rich Pictured Rocks National Lakeshore, the preserve has two waterfalls in canyonlike locations. Also included are northern woods and cliffs, with ferns, a beech grove, and woodland grasses. Michigan Nature Association.

Chippewa County

Roach Point Nature Sanctuary (336 acres) via Gogomain Road, Raber Township. An irregularly shaped peninsula jutting out into the south side of Munuscong Lake, the preserve includes a marsh, muskrat pools, black terns, nesting bald eagles, and threatened plants. Michigan Nature Association.

Keweenaw County

Estivant Pines Sanctuary (378 acres) south of Copper Harbor via Burma Road, Grant Township. Crossed by the Montreal River, the preserve is best known for its 100-foot Estivant pines, more than 5,000 of which remain. There is a loop trail through the trees. In addition to birds, native orchids, virgin cedar, and ferns, old mine workings are visible. Michigan Nature Association.

Luce County

Sleeper Lake Sanctuary (240 acres) northwest of Newberry via County Road 37, McMillan Township. Nesting habitat for sandhill cranes, spruce grouse, solitary vireos, gray jays, and other birds. There is a prime sphagnum bog. Michigan Audubon Society.

Schoolcraft County

Riverbank Sanctuary (23 acres) northwest of Manistique via County Road 440, Hiawatha Township. A typical white cedar bog with abundant wildflowers, spruce, birch, aspen, tamarack, and pine, as well as black bear, deer, and small mammals. It is along the Indian River. Michigan Audubon Society.

FREE VIEW: FIVE LAKES MUSKEGON NATURE SANCTUARY, MUSKEGON

I almost missed the Five Lakes Muskegon Nature Sanctuary, failing to see the small, blink-and-you-miss-it sign that marks the entrance to this secluded 53-acre area. Like many such sanctuaries and preserves, it tries for a low profile to avoid hordes of visitors who might inadvertently— through overuse or carelessness—damage what needs protection.

On an early spring afternoon, I parked alongside some industrial property across the road and followed the trail behind the sign to the heart of the sanctuary. Dried oak leaves made crackle-crunch sounds as I walked through a grove of hardwoods into a prairie, its yellow grasses still swish-dry from the winter. The day was bright enough for sunglasses, cool enough for gloves.

The forces of nature are not static but ever-changing, sometimes slowly, sometimes rapidly. What was a single large lake here in 1836 shrank to five small lakes over the next 140 years. Two of them had virtually disappeared into the sandy soil by the time the Michigan Nature Association bought its first five acres in 1975, but the Five Lakes name remains.

As I walked alone, two red-wing blackbirds called to each other, one perched in a shrub by the lake shore, the other high on a dead oak. Wind-driven ripples marked the surface of the shallow lake, and wind-driven leaves scratched meandering patterns in the sand. I heard the mallards before I saw them, then paused to watch them swoop low over the water.

Rare plants were first known to be collected and identified here in 1900, and the state Natural Features Inventory later designated it as the preserve with the greatest number of endangered, threatened, and special concern plant species, according to the Michigan Nature Association.

"This is the place that stumps the experts," the association says. "It is full of obscure grasses, sedges, rushes, and other weedy looking plants that turn out not to be weeds at all but native species that are some of the most unusual in the state." Many, including the umbrella sedge and the meadow beauty, are generally found only along the Atlantic coast, far away.

Marsh hawks and bluebirds live here, as do herons and woodchucks, salamanders and hog-nosed snakes.

While changes in the geology of the lakes are perceptible only in years or decades, this is a place where "every two weeks or so there is a complete change, with different plants to steal the show," as the association describes it.

> First there is the season of the orange puccoon, then bird's foot violets sparkling like jewels. Lupine weed, the show of wild sweet crab and goat's rue. Late August for the meadow beauty and threatened liggett's pinweed. The prairie comes into its own late, with grasses galore and fields of blazing stars. The end of September is the time for identification of seeds of dozens of grasses, sedges, and bulrushes.

Not all was idyllic, however. Along one trail, I was disturbed to find mounds of junk—tires, a faded dog dish half-filled with rain water, rusting oil cans, a corroded muffin pan partly encrusted with moss, and chrome car parts reflecting the sun.

Five Lakes Muskegon Nature Sanctuary. (Photo by author.)

I heard no clock ticking as I walked, watched, and listened.

I stopped to examine a small nest of grass, leaves, and rootlets, a legacy of last year's hatchlings, wedged into a budding bush. I sat by the side of a partly overgrown pond, enjoying a croaker concert and the guest solos of an unseen bird in a distant tree. The noise of an airplane interrupted like a rude patron half-whispering a joke during a symphony performance, then faded into nothingness. Closing my eyes, I faced into the sun and relished the warmth of another spring and the marvels the season brings to places like these.

Chapter 3
National Wildlife Refuges

Wildlife refuges are meant for passive recreation. Human visitors are expected to leave few footprints and make little noise. They are intended for quiet strokes of a canoe paddle rather than the revving of an outboard motor. Guests should be sensitive to environmental needs and willing to exercise self-restraint.

There are two major national wildlife refuges in Michigan: Seney in the Upper Peninsula and Shiawassee near Saginaw Bay. Both manage smaller satellite refuges. They are part of the U.S. Fish and Wildlife Service's system of about 450 refuges with more than 90 million acres of water and land dedicated to wildlife protection and preservation.

UPPER PENINSULA

Seney National Wildlife Refuge   (906) 586-9851
HCR 2, Box 1
Seney MI 49883

The area now occupied by the 95,455-acre Seney preserve had been lumbered over and then unsuccessfully farmed before it was designated a refuge in 1935. The Civilian Conservation Corps built a system of dikes, ditches, and water control structures that impound more than 7,000 acres of open water in 21 major pools. The refuge includes a 25,000-acre wilderness area. Peak waterfowl populations, such as Canada geese, hooded mergansers, mallards, and ring-necked ducks are present in late summer and fall; sandhill cranes can be seen prior to fall migration. Please remember, wildlife have the right-of-way and be especially careful of geese and goslings on the dikes.

Free Activities and Attractions
- The visitor center, open daily from May 15 to September 30, features exhibits about refuge history, management, and ecology. There is a

children's "touch table" with objects from nature. Movies are shown in the auditorium during the summer, and the staff leads guided programs.
- Bicycling is allowed on a network of 70 miles of roads that are closed to motor vehicles.
- Pine Ridge Nature Trail, 1.4 miles long, provides a look at refuge habitat, wildlife, and plants.
- Marshland Wildlife Drive is a 7-mile self-guided auto tour. Highlights include a wildlife viewing area and eagle observation deck.
- Canoeing and kayaking are allowed on the Manistique, Driggs, and Creighton rivers and Walsh Creek, but not on the marshes or pools. Motor boats can use only the Manistique River. There is no swimming or camping.
- Fishing is permitted during regular state seasons on the Ditch, Creighton, Driggs, and Manistique rivers and Walsh Creek (with a state license). Fishing also is allowed on most pools from May 15 through September 30, and from Labor Day through September 30 on some other pools; a few are off-limits to fishing. Ice fishing is allowed on all pools from January 1 to February 28.

Seney National Wildlife Refuge. (Courtesy U.S. Fish and Wildlife Service.)

- Much of the refuge is open to the picking of morel mushrooms, blueberries, and other wild fruits and foods.
- Cross-country skiing and snowshoeing are allowed, with some trails groomed.

Huron Islands National Wildlife Refuge   (906) 586-9851
c/o Seney National Wildlife Refuge
HCR 2, Box 1
Seney MI 49883

The remote Huron Islands Refuge in Lake Superior between Marquette and the Keweenaw Peninsula contains 147 acres on eight islands and has been designated a wilderness area. West Huron, or Lighthouse, Island is the second largest and the only one open to the public. The lighthouse, now on the National Register of Historic Places, was built in 1877 and automated in 1972. You must register at refuge headquarters to visit the island for hiking or nature study; access is allowed during daylight hours only.

Harbor Island National Wildlife Refuge   (906) 586-9851
c/o Seney National Wildlife Refuge
HCR 2, Box 1
Seney MI 49883

The 695-acre Harbor Island refuge is in Lake Huron's Potagannissing Bay, 1.0 mile north of Drummond Island and 3.5 miles south of the Michigan-Ontario border. It was purchased from the Nature Conservancy as a waterfowl production area under the Unique Ecosystem Program. There is a sheltered bay for boaters for fishing, water skiing, and overnight anchorage. A sandy beach is suitable for swimming.

LOWER PENINSULA

Shiawassee National Wildlife Refuge   (517) 777-5930
6975 Mower Road
Route 1
Saginaw MI 48601

NATIONAL WILDLIFE REFUGES

The Shiawassee refuge is a breeding and stopover area for migratory waterfowl. Established in 1953, it combines wetlands, controlled pools, woods, and cropland, yet is surrounded by industrial development and commercial farms. The Tittabaswasee, Shiawassee, Flint, and Cass rivers and Swan and Bullhead creeks border, touch, or cut through the refuge. Peak migration seasons are March through April and September through November, when up to 25,000 Canada geese and 50,000 ducks can be seen.

Free Activities and Attractions
- Boating, canoeing, fishing, and kayaking are allowed. There is no swimming or camping.
- The 5-mile Waterfowl Trail, part of the flood control dike system, shows strip crop planting, native plants, dead elms, waterfowl feeding areas,

Seney National Wildlife Refuge. (Courtesy U.S. Fish and Wildlife Service.)

the "Green Tree Reservoir" where forestland is flooded each spring to hold waterfowl feed, and "sharecropping" fields where farmers leave part of their crops to feed migratory waterfowl. There is also a 1.5 mile short loop of this trail, as well as other trails and an environmental study area.

Chapter 4

Nature Centers

Nature centers serve as focal points for both environmental education and such environmentally friendly activities as walking, cross-country skiing, birdwatching, and photography. Many have natural history library collections, and trained naturalists are always happy to answer questions and provide information. Although some programs put on by the centers are restricted to school or camp groups, most are open to the public. Trails are marked, with trail maps generally available at the interpretive center.

Excluded are nature centers located in state and regional parks that charge a park admission fee, even if there is no added charge to visit the center.

The listings indicate whether a center offers any free tours, classes, or other programs/lectures, although there may be a fee for some of these activities. Codes are Y (yes) and N (no).

SOUTHEAST

Jackson County

Dahlem Environmental Education Center 7117 S. Jackson Road Jackson MI 49201	(517) 782-3453 Year-round Tues.–Fri., 8–5	N	N	N

Located on an ecologically diverse 300-acre site, the center features five miles of trails through woods, fields, marshland, and native prairie. The visitor building is located in an arboretum and offers interactive exhibits, living life-cycle displays, and an observation bee hive. Trails are open every day, and there are special needs trails for visitors with disabilities.

Macomb County

Sterling Heights Nature Center 42700 Utica Road Box 8009 Sterling Heights MI 48313	(313) 739-6731 Year-round Sun.–Thurs., 1–5 Saturday, 10–5	Y	N	Y

Located on the main branch of the Clinton River, the site includes six miles of paved trails for hiking or bicycling. The exhibit room features live Michigan reptiles and amphibians, plus mounted mammals and birds. There are nature films, campfires, guided walks, lectures, and guest travelogues. Operated by city of Sterling Heights.

Oakland County

Dinosaur Hill Nature Preserve 333 N. Hill Circle Rochester MI 48307	(313) 656-0999 Year-round Monday, 9–2 Tues.–Fri., 9–5 Weekends, Noon–3	N	N	N

This preserve includes a small nature center and interpretive center.

Drayton Plains Nature Center 2125 Denby Drive Drayton Plains MI 48329	(313) 674-2119 Year-round Weekends, 10–4	N	N	N

The 137-acre site includes ponds, a waterfowl rehabilitation area, woods, a duck-feeding area, interpretive center, and a special nature trail for the blind and visually impaired. Special events include an Earth Day open house.

E. L. Johnson Nature Center 3325 Franklin Road Bloomfield Hills MI 48302	(313) 540-5291 Year-round Mon.–Fri., dawn to dusk	N	N	N

The 32-acre site boasts rolling terrain with a diversity of wildflowers and trees. Wildlife includes red fox, blue herons, geese, ducks, and woodchucks. Deer, owls, and red-tailed hawks can be seen in large pens. A stream borders the property, and there's a spring-fed pond. There's also a log cabin and outdoor amphitheater. The center hosts an annual Maple Sugar Tap. Operated by Bloomfield Hills School District.

Hess-Hathaway Park 825 S. Williams Lake Road Waterford MI 48327	(313) 360-3814 Year-round June–August, Daily 9–8 September–May, Daily 10–5	N	N	N

This 165-acre park emphasizes Michigan's agricultural heritage. Known as Lone Cedar Farms and describing itself as a "working museum," it includes a historic farmhouse and farm animal exhibit barn, as well as nature trails for hiking and cross-country skiing. Operated by Waterford Township Parks and Recreation Department.

Lloyd A. Stage Outdoor Education Center 6685 Coolidge Highway Troy MI 48098	(313) 524-3567 Year-round Tues.–Sat., 8:30–4:30 Sunday, Noon–5	Y	N	Y

With 99 acres of forest, meadow, and marsh along the north branch of the Rouge River, most natural communities of southeastern Michigan can be seen as you walk along its nature trails. The center is home to foxes, weasels, raccoons, white-tailed deer, and woodchucks; more than 150 species of birds have been seen here. Wildflowers include orchids, trillium, and columbine. There are displays and games in the interpretive building. Special events include Maple Syrup Time, Wildflower Weekend, and Nature's Harvest Weekend. Operated by Troy Parks and Recreation Department.

Wayne County

Anna Scripps Whitcomb Conservatory Belle Isle Park Detroit MI 48207	(313) 267-7133 Year-round Wed.–Sun., 9–5	Y	N	N

This tropical plant conservatory grows palms, ferns, desert plants, fruit trees, and orchids. From May through frost, visitors can see roses, other

Anna Scripps Whitcomb Conservatory. (Photo by author.)

perennials, annual flower beds, and a water lily pool outside. The conservatory also boasts one of the world's largest floral clocks, 25 feet in diameter. Seasonal flower exhibits include Easter, Mother's Day, summer, chrysanthemum, and Christmas shows. Operated by Detroit Recreation Department.

Belle Isle Nature Center	(313) 267-7157	Y	Y	Y
Belle Isle Park	Year-round			
Detroit MI 48207	Wed.–Sun., 10–4			

The center features a collection of Michigan live reptiles and amphibians, a 250-acre nature area with trails, and a series of museum-type displays, some of them interactive. There is a weekly Sunday afternoon series of nature programs. Special events include Earth Week, Winter Fest, and an October "haunted forest."

SOUTHWEST

Berrien County

Sarett Nature Center	(616) 927-4832	Y	Y	Y
2300 Benton Center Road	Year-round			
Benton Harbor MI 49022	Tues.–Fri., 9–5			
	Saturday, 10–5			
	Sunday, 1–5			

There are more than five miles of trails on 350 acres of upland meadows, dry forest, marshes, and swamp forest. Special events include Maple Sugar Day, naturalist-led walks, and nature videos.

Kent County

Blandford Nature Center	(616) 453-6192	N	N	N
1715 Hillburn N.W.	Year-round			
Grand Rapids MI 49504	Mon.–Fri., 9–5			
	Weekends, 1–5			

This 143-acre site includes trails through marshes, creeks, mature forests, and old fields. A Heritage Complex and Farmstead highlight late nineteenth-century life through a one-room schoolhouse, blacksmith shop, cabin, and carriage barn. The interpretive building features exhibits and the Wildlife Care Center, which rehabilitates injured wildlife. There is a paved trail for the physically challenged near the interpretive building. Special events include Sugarbush, Civil War Days, and a Fall Earth Festival. Operated by the Grand Rapids Public Museum.

Howard Christensen Nature Center (616) 887-1852   N N N
16160 Red Pine Drive   Year-round
Kent City MI 49330   Mon.–Fri., 8–4:30

Nature trails range from 0.2 to 1.5 miles in length and pass by a variety of habitats including pine and spruce plantations, a tadpole pond, bog, hardwood swamp, and coniferous wetland forest. Although the building is open only during the week, visitors can use the grounds on weekends as well. Operated by Kent Intermediate School District.

Ottawa County

De Graaf Nature Center   (616) 396-2739   Y N Y
600 Graafschap Road   Year-round
Holland MI 49423   Weekdays, 11–4:30
                            Weekends, 2–4

There is a series of trails on this 15-acre site, traversing marsh, wetlands, meadow, woodlands, and a butterfly garden. A log cabin stands by the herb garden. A solar-heated interpretive center displays Michigan rocks, stuffed animals, a wall mural diorama, and changing displays. Special events include Maple Sugar Community Day, Baby Animal Day, and Pioneer Christmas.

CENTRAL

Genesee County

For-Mar Nature Preserve and   (313) 789-8548   N N N
  Arboretum   Year-round
G-5360 E. Potter Road   Daily, 8–Sunset
Burton MI 48506

There are miles of hiking trails through the 380-acre site, which includes a 113-acre arboretum. On the grounds are demonstration gardens and a windmill. The interpretive center houses the Croyden Foote Bird Collection. Operated by the Genesee County Parks and Recreation Commission.

NATURE CENTERS

Ligon Outdoor Center   (313) 687-4270   Y   Y   Y
5213 E. Farrand Road   Year-round
Clio MI 48420   Mon.–Fri., 8–4

Diverse ecosystems here include a 5-acre lake, conifer and deciduous forests, meadow, and wetlands. There's also a network of walking trails, plus picnic areas and a large floating dock at Lake Ligon. Special events include an annual Earth Day celebration and open house programs. Operated by the Genesee Intermediate School District.

Ingham County

Carl G. Fenner Arboretum   (517) 483-4224   N   N   Y
2020 E. Mt. Hope   Year-round
Lansing MI 48910   Tues.–Fri., 9–4
                              Saturday, 10–5
                              Sunday, 11–5

Five miles of trails wind through different habitats in the arboretum's 120 acres, with its orchard, oak uplands, marshy thicket, swamp forest, pine plantations, and maple grove. There are two ponds, wildlife feeding stations, and a carved wooden totem pole, as well as a replica of a nineteenth-century pioneer log cabin and typical kitchen garden of that period. A live bison is on the grounds. The nature center building includes interpretive displays, children's activities, and native birds, reptiles, and amphibians, plus a natural history library. Special programs include an Apple Butter Festival and Maple Syrup Festival. The grounds are open daily from 8 A.M. until dusk.

Livingston County

Howell Nature Center   (517) 546-0249   N   N   N
1005 Triangle Lake Road   Year-round
Howell MI 48843   Mon.–Fri., 9–5
                              Weekends, 1–4

This 270-acre nature center presents a special attraction, a wildlife rehabilitation facility that each year takes care of more than 500 injured, orphaned, or sick animals and birds, including deer, foxes, hawks, coyotes, eagles, raccoons, waterfowl, possums, ferrets, and songbirds.

Midland County

Chippewa Nature Center	(517) 631-0830	N N Y
400 S. Badour Road	Year-round	
Midland MI 48640	Mon.–Fri., 8–5	
	Saturday, 9–5	
	Sunday, 1–5	

The center owns 1,000 acres of woods, fields, ponds, rivers, and wetlands, with an arboretum of Michigan trees and shrubs. Twelve miles of trails are open during daylight hours for hiking and cross-country skiing. The visitor center includes a museum of Saginaw Valley cultural and geological history, wildlife viewing and feeding station, and wildflower walkway. An 1870s homestead farm, open Sunday afternoons from April through October, features live animals, a log schoolhouse, gardens of herbs and heirloom vegetables, and costumed interpreters who lead hands-on activities. A sugarhouse for maple syrup production is open in March.

NORTHEAST

Presque Isle County

Hammond Bay Biological Station	(517) 734-4768	Y N N
U.S. Fish and Wildlife Service	Year-round	
11188 Ray Road	Mon.–Fri., 1–3	
Millersburg MI 49759		

This federally run research and laboratory facility specializes in the problems of sea lampreys, an invader that threatens sport and commercial fishing in the Great Lakes. Laboratory tours show the life stages of sea lampreys and present a brief history of the sea lamprey control program in the Great Lakes.

NORTHWEST

Manistee County

Lake Bluff Audubon Center (616) 723-4042   Y Y Y
2890 Lakeshore Road   July–September
Box 772   Saturday, Noon–4
Manistee MI 49660

The grounds occupy one-third of a mile of bluff overlooking Lake Michigan. Its arboretum is landscaped with Michigan and nonnative shrubs and trees, including California redwoods. In addition, there's a 40-acre woodlot and several trails, including a nature trail that begins behind the stables. Environmental displays are in the Gray House, which is only open on Saturday afternoons during the summer. However, the grounds remain open year-round. Tours of the house and grounds are offered, along with nature walks and guest speakers. Operated by Michigan Audubon Society.

Chapter 5

National Forests

Although many people envision auto factories and steel plants, bean fields and dairy farms, or racing yachts and sandy Great Lakes beaches when they think about Michigan, the reality is that national forests cover much of the Upper Peninsula and the northern half of the Lower Peninsula. Together, they account for more than 2.7 million acres, roughly 14.5 percent of all private and public forestland in Michigan.

While one major purpose for their establishment by Congress was to serve the timber industry, national forestland also provides opportunities for uncrowded recreation, some remote, others easily accessible by motor vehicle. In particular, national forests are ideal for boating, canoeing, hiking, fishing, camping, cross-country skiing, swimming, and even exploring history.

With the exception of most organized campgrounds and a few boat launches, there's generally no charge for using national forests in Michigan. Camping in the backcountry—so-called dispersed camping—is free; visitors may find fire rings and a tent-sized cleared area at some locations, but no drinking water, sanitary facilities, or picnic table.

LOWER PENINSULA

Huron-Manistee National Forests

421 S. Mitchell St.	(800) 821-6263
Cadillac MI 49601	(616) 775-2421
Baldwin Ranger District	(616) 745-4631
Cadillac Ranger District	(616) 775-8539
Harrisville Ranger District	(517) 724-5431
Manistee Ranger District	(616) 723-2211
Mio Ranger District	(517) 826-3252
Tawas Ranger District	(517) 362-4477
White Cloud Ranger District	(616) 689-6696

NATIONAL FORESTS

The Huron-Manistee National Forests are two geographically separate entities that are jointly administered.

The Huron portion is located in the northeastern part of the Lower Peninsula, between the South Branch of the Au Sable River and Lake Huron near Oscoda. Its 432,836 acres include a variety of waterways and a statue in memory of Michigan's pioneer lumberers of the 1800s.

The Manistee portion, primarily in the northwestern part of the Lower Peninsula, reaches Lake Michigan north of Muskegon. Its 531,085 acres also boast a wealth of rivers, streams, and lakes.

Free Attractions
- The 1932 Lumberman's Monument west of Oscoda is a 14-foot-high bronze statue of a sawyer, a river driver, a timber cruiser, and their tools. Their labors "made possible the development of the prairie states," according to the inscription.
- The adjacent visitor center has outdoor exhibits that explain how logs are cut and transported to sawmills, as well as slide shows, a book shop, and a 260-step stairway down to scenic Cooke Pond.
- Just to the west of the visitor center is Eagle's Nest Overlook, where bald eagles have nested since about 1985. Binoculars are recommended.
- Also nearby, the Kiwanis Monument honors Kiwanis clubs in Michigan for donating money in 1928 to plant 10,000 acres of red pines.
- Hundreds of miles of marked canoeing, cross-country skiing, snowmobile, hiking, motorcycle, off-road vehicle, and horseback trails cross a variety of terrains, ranging from generally flat to sharply hilly. The North Country National Scenic Trail, Shore-to-Shore Trail, and the Michigan Cross Country Cycle Trail cross the Huron-Manistee National Forests.
- Guided tours of Kirtland's warbler nesting areas leave from Mio and Grayling from mid-May through early July. Late May and June are recommended for the best chances of spotting these rare songbirds. The national forest includes a 4,010-acre Kirtland's Warbler Management Area. Participants are encouraged to bring binoculars or spotting scopes but cannot play recorded warbler singing. For more information, contact the District Ranger, Huron National Forest, Mio MI 48647, (517) 826-3252, or the U.S. Fish and Wildlife Service, East Lansing Field Office, 1405 S. Harrison Road, East Lansing MI 48823, (517) 337-6650.

- There are self-guided nature trails, such as the Island Lake Nature Trail between Rose City and Mio.
- Mushroom gathering is popular from late April through June. Morels, puff balls, and shaggy manes are the most plentiful of the edible ones.
- Loda Lake Wild Flower Sanctuary northwest of White Cloud preserves native Michigan plants, supported by the Federated Garden Clubs of Michigan donations. There are marked trails, a trail guide, and a picnic area (for more details, see chap. 2).
- Cooper Creek Grouse Management Area, a joint project of the U.S. Forest Service and Ruffed Grouse Society of North America. Habitat work and selective cuttings of alders and noncommercial aspen, coupled with planting of food-bearing shrubs, have been performed to make the area more hospitable to grouse.

UPPER PENINSULA

Hiawatha National Forest

2727 N. Lincoln Road (906) 786-4062
Escanaba MI 48929

Manistique Ranger District	(906) 341-5666
Munising Ranger District	(906) 387-2512
Rapid River Ranger District	(906) 474-6442
Sault Ste. Marie Ranger District	(906) 635-5311
St. Ignace Ranger District	(906) 643-7900

Hiawatha National Forest covers 860,000 acres in the eastern and central Upper Peninsula. It touches three of the Great Lakes—Huron, Michigan, and Superior—as well as many inland lakes, rivers, and streams such as the Au Train, Sturgeon, Whitefish, and Carp rivers. Wildlife includes black bear, moose, whitetail deer, bobcats, and coyotes. Sand dunes, pine plantations, and agate-strewn beaches are among the natural features.

Free Attractions
- Hundreds of miles of marked trails for hiking, canoeing, horseback riding, cross-country skiing, and snowmobiling. Crossing the national forest is the North Country Hiking Trail, which stretches from New York to North Dakota. There are also bicycle routes.

- Remnants of the past are evident, such as the iron kiln ruins of Onota, an iron smelting town near Munising from 1869–77, and the sites of Depression-era Civilian Conservation Corps camps, several of which housed German military prisoners during World War II (for more information on CCC auto routes, see chap. 14).
- At Peninsula Point south of Stonington, visitors can climb a circular staircase to the top of a 40-foot lighthouse tower finished in 1865 and used until 1936. The reward is a spectacular view of Lake Michigan. There's also a picnic area at Peninsula Point, where thousands of monarch butterflies rest before migrating across Green Bay each fall.
- At Point Iroquois northwest of Brimley, the 1870 brick lighthouse is now a museum and visitor center, with a 65-foot spiral staircase. From the top, visitors can watch ships pass through the Soo locks (for more information on the museum, see chap. 8).
- The Round Island lighthouse, built in 1895 and abandoned in 1847, is easily visible from Mackinac Island and the Mackinac Bridge. Round Island is a designated wilderness area and is accessible only by private boat.
- Pendills Creek Fish Hatchery, which restocks lake trout for the Great Lakes, is open to the public. West of Sault Ste. Marie near Whitefish Bay, it is run by the U.S. Fish and Wildlife Service (for more information on the hatchery, see chap. 7). Nearby is Salt Point, where the shattered ribs of a sunken salt barge are visible just offshore.
- There are several designated wilderness areas with few trails, if any, in the national forest. For example, in Big Island Lake Wilderness, hikers can explore the remains of old logging campsites and a homestead. Former logging roads are evident within Delirium Wilderness. Two abandoned railroad grades cut through Rock River Canyon. And 20-foot-high Sturgeon Falls was formed by volcanic rock outcrops at Sturgeon River Gorge Wilderness. Motor vehicles and motorized equipment are not allowed in wilderness areas.

Ottawa National Forest

East U.S. 2
Ironwood MI 49938

(800) 562-1201
(906) 932-1330

Bessemer Ranger District
Bergland Ranger District

(906) 667-0261
(906) 575-3441

Iron River Ranger District	(906) 265-5139
Kenton Ranger District	(906) 852-3501
Ontonagon Ranger District	(906) 884-2085
Watersmeet Ranger District	(906) 358-4551

Ottawa National Forest is in the western Upper Peninsula, bordering Lake Superior. Its 954,000 acres include 2,000 miles of stream, more than 700 lakes, a variety of waterfalls, and picturesque Black River Harbor.

Free Attractions
- Black River Harbor is the site of an old fishing village and small boat harbor on Lake Superior at the mouth of the Black River, about 15 miles north of Bessemer. It's one of only two harbors within the national forest system. A foot suspension bridge leads to the beach and Rainbow Falls.
- The U.S. Forest Service calls this Waterfall Country. Many falls are accessible by trails, but visitors need a map and compass to find others. Among them are 40-foot Rainbow Falls, 40-foot Conglomerate Falls, 24-foot Gorge Falls, and 30-foot Potawatomi Falls.
- Hikers and backpackers will find nearly 200 miles of marked trails, including 118 challenging miles of the North Country National Scenic Trail that, when complete, will run 3,200 miles between the Appalachian Trail in Vermont and the Lewis and Clark Trail in North Dakota. The Stateline National Recreation Trail marks the only stretch of Upper Peninsula nonwater state border; along the route are a tree stump and marker indicating where two treaties were signed with local Indians to protect nineteenth-century surveyors measuring that border.
- For those who enjoy canoeing with history, the Brule River, which flows between Michigan and Wisconsin, was used by early surveyors and traders. Ottawa National Forest has a plentitude of other canoeing opportunities on its 1,800 miles of streams and rivers and its 500-plus lakes.
- Wildernesses include McCormick Wilderness, formerly used as a vacation retreat by descendants of reaper inventor Cyrus McCormick, and site of the McCormick Research Natural Area; Sturgeon River Gorge Wilderness, with volcanic outcrops, waterfalls, and steep, rugged terrain; and Sylvania Wilderness, home to rare orchids, bald eagles, loons, and osprey, as well as archaeological explorations into prehistoric activity.

FREE VIEW: MACKENZIE SKI TRAILS, CADILLAC

Except for the soft whoosh-whoosh of my skis, all's quiet beneath the pines as a gentle wind dislodges newly fallen snow from the branches above. The gray-white bark of leafless birches contrasts with the glistening whiteness of the surrounding snow.

This is one of the four MacKenzie Ski Trails, which stretch almost 13 miles in the Huron-Manistee National Forest, about 15 miles west of Cadillac.

National forestland in Michigan offers hundreds of miles of marked ski trails. Like others, the MacKenzie trails combine the outdoor experiences, serenity, and a lack of crowds that can make cross-country skiing so appealing, so unstressful, so much attuned to the environment. That means most cross-country trails through the national forests don't attract skiers who relish the amenities of convenient hot meals and chalet-style socializing.

Yet unlike most such trails, such luxuries are immediately at hand because the MacKenzie trails are adjacent to Caberfae, the popular downhill ski resort, with its T-bars, chair lifts, rope tows, snowmaking equipment, and dozens of runs down the mountain. You can park free at Caberfae and use its cafeterias, snack bar, and restrooms. If you don't have your own cross-country gear, it's available for rent.

There are marked trail heads for each of the MacKenzie routes: west of Edelweiss Lodge at the bottom of the beginner downhill hill; north of Sky View Cafeteria; at the southwest corner of the Caberfae Way Snowmobile Trail parking lot; and on 38 Road, 0.75 miles west of the entrance to the downhill area.

Despite the proximity of Caberfae, you're more likely to spot a deer or rabbit than a stranger along some stretches of the trail. The solitude provides an opportunity to wonder what makes the translucent dead leaves stubbornly cling to otherwise winter-bare branches, to fantasize about how far you could go off the trail in some direction before finding a road or a house.

To help skiers, the MacKenzie trails are marked for difficulty with diamond-shaped blazers on trees and posts. There's a "You Are Here" map posted at each intersection, showing your present location and the rest of the trails. If you want to rest or picnic, you'll even find benches at several of the intersections.

It's important to know your own stamina and that of your companions.

Sudden bad weather, fatigue, a twisted ankle, or changing snow conditions can make a route much longer than it appears on the map. Plan ahead to give yourself plenty of time to return before darkness sets in. First aid is available at Caberfae.

Use a fanny pack to carry snacks, water, a plastic ski tip, compass, matches, wax for changing snow conditions, and extra gloves and socks. Be sure to drink plenty of water: just because it's cold doesn't mean you won't sweat.

Chapter 6

Outdoor Opportunities

Michigan has an outdoor orientation, promoting its woodlands, sand dunes, waters, mountains, and other natural resources as places for recreation. Best of all, access to free opportunities is easy regardless of whether you visit or live in the state. Public land and public access sites are found in Detroit and other cities as well as in suburbs and rural areas.

STATE FORESTS

Michigan boasts 3.9 million acres of state-owned forestland, forming the largest forest system of any state. Their acreage accounts for 21 percent of Michigan's public and private forestland. State forests contain many noncontiguous pieces scattered across multiple counties. For instance, parts of the Au Sable State Forest are located in nine mid-Michigan and northern counties in the Lower Peninsula.

With the exception of camping at developed campgrounds, there is generally no fee for using state forests, including their boat launches, fishing, hiking and cross-country ski trails, picnic areas, beaches, and backcountry camping. Special attractions include interpretive pathways, historic sites, and scenic vistas. As examples, visitors can hunt for agates on the beach near Lake Superior Forest Campground east of Grand Marais or see a Civilian Conservation Corps historic site near Pickerel Lake Forest Campground east of Vanderbilt. Or you can observe the biggest elk herd east of the Mississippi at the Gaylord Area Wildlife Viewing Area northeast of Gaylord, with nine designated viewing sites; dawn and dusk are the recommended times for spotting the herd.

For more information, contact the Department of Natural Resources, Forest Management Division, Box 30028, Lansing MI 48909, (517) 373-1275.

Lower Peninsula

Au Sable State Forest
191 S. Mt. Tom Road
Mio MI 48647

(517) 826-3211
748,458 acres

Mackinaw State Forest
Box 667
Gaylord MI 49735

(517) 732-3541
663,843 acres

Pere Marquette State Forest
8015 Mackinaw Trail
Cadillac MI 49601

(616) 775-9727
621,052 acres

Upper Peninsula

Copper Country State Forest
U.S. 41 North, Box 440
Baraga MI 49908

(906) 353-6651
430,291 acres

Escanaba River State Forest
6833 Highway 2
Gladstone MI 49837

(906) 786-2351
402,696 acres

Lake Superior State Forest
309 W. McMillan Ave.
Newberry MI 49868

(906) 293-5131
1,026,058 acres

CANOEING, KAYAKING, AND BOATING

If you own or can borrow a canoe, kayak, or boat, there are more than 1,200 public boat launches across the state. That number grows as more access sites are acquired with marine fuel taxes and boat registration fees. You'll find them on the Great Lakes and hundreds of inland lakes and rivers, in urban areas and in Michigan's remotest regions. Most are administered by the Department of Natural Resources, with the rest operated by other government agencies or local communities. Most charge no fee. For a free directory of boat launch sites, contact the DNR Recreation Division, Box 30028, Lansing MI 48909, (517) 373-9900. A complete list appears in *On the Water, Michigan: Your Comprehensive Guide to Water Recreation in the Great Lake State*, by Eric Freedman (Huron-Superior-Michigan Press).

CROSS-COUNTRY SKIING

Where? Almost anywhere. For easy terrain, try a golf course or local park. For more challenges, head for state or national forestland. Hiking trails and logging roads are generally well marked, and many are groomed.

The Department of Natural Resources has a series of mapped, marked pathways through the state forests. For maps, contact the Forest Management Division, Box 30028, Lansing MI 48909, (517) 373-1275. Another popular ski area with excellent cross-country trails is Sleeping Bear Dunes National Lakeshore. For a brochure, contact Superintendent, Sleeping Bear Dunes National Lakeshore, Box 277, Empire MI 49630, (616) 326-5134.

Belle Isle Canoeing. (Courtesy Michigan Travel Bureau.)

UNDERWATER PRESERVES

If you enjoy scuba diving, Michigan has the nation's most comprehensive system of bottomland preserves, created to protect Great Lakes shipwrecks and natural features. A network of nine preserves covers 1,650 square miles of Lakes Superior, Huron, and Michigan. The state has strict laws against vandalism and unauthorized removal or destruction of underwater artifacts. These protected areas are the resting places of more than 100 known shipwrecks, some deeply submerged and others in water shallow enough to be explored with only a mask and snorkel. There are no fees for diving in the preserves.

Northeast

Thunder Bay Preserve	289 square miles	Lake Huron
Sanilac Shores Preserve	160 square miles	Lake Huron
Thumb Area Preserve	276 square miles	Lake Huron

Northwest

Manitou Passage Preserve	281 square miles	Lake Michigan

Upper Peninsula

Alger Preserve	113 square miles	Lake Superior
Keweenaw Preserve	192 square miles	Lake Superior
Marquette Preserve	174 square miles	Lake Superior
Straits of Mackinac Preserve	152 square miles	Lakes Huron and Michigan
Whitefish Point Preserve	375 square miles	Lake Superior

For more information, contact the Michigan Underwater Salvage and Preserve Committee, Department of Natural Resources, Box 30028, Lansing MI 48909, (517) 373-1950, or Michigan Underwater Preserve Council, c/o Mike Kohut, 4424 N. Woodward Ave., Royal Oak MI 48073, (313) 549-0303.

Diving in a Great Lakes underwater preserve. (Courtesy Michigan State University.)

STATE GAME AND WILDLIFE AREAS

State game and wildlife areas are scattered across Michigan. Much of the land comes from funds raised from or donated by hunters and hunting groups, but you need not be a hunter or trapper to enjoy them. They offer trails for hiking, snowshoeing, and cross-country skiing, as well as habitats ideal for photography, birdwatching, and nature study. Canoeing and fishing are allowed on lakes and streams, except in restricted sections.

Certain land is set aside as nature refuges, which require special authorization for access. The Allegan State Game Area's Fennville Farm is a 1,300-acre refuge for Canada geese, eagles, and other migrating birds. The 1,109-acre Nayanquing Point Wildlife Area at Tobisco Marsh State Game Area near Bay City features waterfowl, songbirds, rare wildflowers, mink, beaver, deer, and muskrat. Other refuges and sanctuaries can be found in the Sturgeon River Sloughs Wildlife Area in the Upper Peninsula, St. Clair Flats Wildlife Area on Harsens Island in the St. Clair River, Pointe Mouillee State Game Area on Lake Erie, Lapeer State Game Area, Fish Point Wildlife Area in Tuscola County, Crow Island State Game Area on the Saginaw River, Leidy Lake State Game Area near Colon, and Grand Haven State Game Area.

DNR wildlife research areas are located at Rose Lake, Houghton Lake, Beaver Island, and Cusino. For dog enthusiasts, there are designated field dog trial spots in the Sharonville State Game Area in Jackson County and at Lapeer State Game Area. For maps and additional information, contact the DNR Wildlife Division, Box 30028, Lansing MI 48909, (517) 373-9311.

LOOKING FOR HAWKS

The Keweenaw Peninsula's Copper Harbor is a regular spring stop for thousands of eager birdwatchers. That's where the free annual Hawk Watch is held. Birders and ornithologists look for migrating American eagles, Cooper's hawks, sharp-shinned hawks, and turkey vultures, among other birds. To improve their sighting chances, participants make the 3.5-mile trip to the summit of Brockway Mountain, often by foot. For more information, call (800) 338-7982 or (906) 289-4652.

LOOKING FOR WATERFOWL

The St. Charles Waterfowl Observatory is on the banks of the Bad River within a wildlife habitat demonstration area. It's at the gateway to the Shiawassee Flats, a 50-square-mile area where waters from 22 counties meet to form the Saginaw River. The area is managed principally for waterfowl resting, feeding, and breeding. The observatory is open from dawn to dusk from May through October. For more information, contact the Village of St. Charles, 110 W. Spruce St., St. Charles MI 48655-1299, (517) 865-8287.

BICYCLING

Take a bicycle and helmet along when you travel. Several factors make Michigan a great place to ride. There's the scenery, of course, as well as an excellent system of secondary and paved back roads and a growing number of designated bike routes. A major plus is the state's 10-cent bottle and can deposit law, which sharply reduces litter and broken glass on the road. The amount of litter is also down due to the popular Adopt-a-Highway program, in which local organizations and businesses provide volunteers to periodically clean "their" stretches of road.

Meanwhile, the rails-to-trails movement is working aggressively to obtain unused railroad rights-of-way for conversion to bike trails, envisioning a statewide network of such routes. The Michigan Department of Transportation has a nonmotorized transportation unit to work with bicyclists. For those who enjoy mountain biking, there are millions of acres of free off-road riding opportunities in the national and state forests and state game areas.

When you're in unfamiliar territory, drop into a local bike shop for suggestions about where to ride, on or off the road. Also, free maps available from county road commissions let you plan your own routes.

Chapter 7
Fishing

Fishing is big recreation and big business in Michigan, a fact that should be of little surprise given the state's prime location, bordering four of the five Great Lakes, and its more than 11,000 inland lakes and 36,350 miles of rivers and streams. The Department of Natural Resources issues an average of 1.2 million annual fishing licenses to residents, nonresidents, and seniors, plus 275,000 one-day permits each year.

There's a free fishing weekend each June, intended to promote fishing resources. For those two days, no licenses or trout stamps are needed to fish the Great Lakes or inland waters. The event coincides with National Fishing Week and often features special activities sponsored by DNR, the U.S. Forest Service, and local sports groups. For more information, contact the Fisheries Division, Department of Natural Resources, Box 30028, Lansing MI 48909, (517) 373-1280.

STATE AND FEDERAL FISH HATCHERIES

The Michigan Department of Natural Resources operates six fish hatcheries that produce many species for release, or planting, into Michigan's lakes and rivers. The U.S. Fish and Wildlife Service operates three more to raise lake trout. These hatcheries are an essential part of the commitment to quality fishing experiences for residents and for visitors.

Hatcheries are open to the public for free, self-guided tours, generally from 8:00 A.M. to 4:00 or 4:30 P.M., depending on the facility and season. Visitors can see fish-raising features such as incubation rooms, indoor rearing tanks, and outdoor rearing raceways. At certain times, visitors also may be able to watch the feeding process and the loading of fish from the raceways onto trucks by hand or by pump.

SOUTHWEST

Van Buren County

Wolf Lake State Fish Hatchery   (616) 668-3388
34270 C.R. 652
Mattawan MI 49071

Main species. Northern pike, Atlantic salmon, rainbow trout, tiger muskellunge, chinook salmon, sturgeon, Montana grayling, muskellunge, walleye, brown trout, channel catfish. Wolf Lake produces 3.5 million fish per year.

The Wolf Lake facility includes a free museum that depicts the history of fisheries in Michigan, the commercial fishing industry, the sea lamprey invasion of the Great Lakes, fishing gear, and some record-breaking specimens. The Michigan Room features dioramas of various fish habitats in the state, such as warm water and trout streams. There are three-dimensional Great Lake charts. Also, there are audiovisual programs

Harrietta State Fish Hatchery. (Courtesy Michigan Department of Natural Resources.)

about fisheries management and hatcheries operations. The museum is closed Mondays and Tuesdays.

NORTHWEST

Antrim County

Jordan River National Fish   (616) 584-2461
  Hatchery
Route 1, Box 64-A
Elmira MI 49730

Main species. Lake trout. Fish raised here are released into Lakes Michigan, Huron, and Superior. There is a visitor center, outdoor kiosk, and self-guided tours. It's 3.5 miles north of Alba off U.S. 131.

Benzie County

Platte River State Fish Hatchery   (616) 325-4611
15210 U.S. 31
Beulah MI 49617

Main species. Coho salmon and chinook salmon. The state's largest hatchery, it raises 7 to 8 million young salmon each year.

Emmet County

Oden State Fish Hatchery   (616) 347-4689
3377$^{1}/_{2}$ Oden Road
Oden MI 49764

Main species. Rainbow trout and brown trout. It produces 1 to 2 million trout each year.

Wexford County

Harrietta State Fish Hatchery   (616) 389-2211
6801 Thirty Mile Road
Harrietta MI 49638

Main species. Rainbow trout and brown trout.

FISHING

UPPER PENINSULA

Chippewa County

Hiawatha Forest National (906) 248-5231
  Fish Hatchery
Rte. 1, Box 4442
Brimley MI 49715

Main species. Lake trout. There are self-guided tours of the hatchery, which raises about 800,000 fry a year. There also is a picnic area. It's on Forest Road 31, five miles southwest of Raco.

Pendills Creek National (906) 437-5231
  Fish Hatchery
Rte. 1, Box 420
Brimley MI 49715

Main species. Lake trout. In addition to self-guided tours, the hatchery has a small visitor center with displays and an outdoor kiosk with photographs describing its operations. It's 18 miles west of Brimley on Lakeshore Drive.

Marquette County

Marquette State Fish Hatchery (906) 249-1611
488 Cherry Creek Road
Marquette MI 49855

Main species. Lake trout, brook trout, splake. It produces 1.7 million fish each year.

Schoolcraft County

Thompson State Fish Hatchery (906) 341-5587
Rte. 2, Box 2555
Manistique MI 49854

Main species. Rainbow trout, brown trout, chinook salmon, walleye. It raises 1 million trout, 16 million walleye, and 500,000 salmon each year. It's on M-149 north of Thompson.

MASTER ANGLER PROGRAM

The Department of Natural Resources operates a free Master Angler program that awards certificates for catching state-record fish or one of the top five fish of its kind for the year. Fish must be weighed on inspected scales, and the signatures of two witnesses and pictures must be submitted. Winners receive arm patches.

Eligible species are: largemouth bass, smallmouth bass, white bass, rock bass, warmouth bass, green sunfish, bluegill, pumpkinseed sunfish, redear sunfish, hybrid sunfish, white crappie, black crappie, walleye, sauger, perch, Great Lakes muskellunge, northern muskellunge, tiger muskellunge, northern pike, channel catfish, flathead catfish, brown bullhead, black bullhead, yellow bullhead, burbot, gar, lake sturgeon, Atlantic salmon, chinook salmon, coho salmon, pink salmon, rainbow trout (steelhead), smelt, largemouth buffalo, brown trout, brook trout, lake trout, splake, bowfin (dogfish), redhorse sucker, white sucker, longnose sucker, hog sucker, carpsucker, carp, freshwater drum, lake whitefish, Menominee whitefish, lake herring cisco, mooneye, and American eel.

Applications are available through DNR offices or the DNR Fisheries Division, Box 30028, Lansing MI 48909, (517) 373-1280.

FREE FISHING SPOTS

There are countless spots for free fishing across Michigan, on the Great Lakes and on inland waters. They include parks without entry fees, state game areas, national parks and forests, roadside rest areas, public access launch sites, and bridges. Dave Richey, an outdoor writer for the *Detroit News,* ranks these as some of his Great Lakes favorites.

Elizabeth Park, Trenton, for walleye, silver bass, smallmouth bass, and perch.

Waterworks Park, Port Huron, for salmon, trout, and walleye.

Port Austin Pier, Port Austin, for coho, chinook salmon, steelhead, perch, brown trout, and walleye.

Harrisville Harbor, Harrisville, for salmon, trout, and perch.

Lake Township Park, Honor, for steelhead and salmon.

Frankfort-Elberta Piers, Frankfort and Elberta, for brown trout, steelhead, and perch.

FISHING

Smelt fishing on Days Creek. (Courtesy Michigan Travel Bureau.)

Thompson Creek Mouth, Thompson, for salmon and trout.
Munising Pier, Munising, for salmon, trout, menominee, and whitefish.
Second Sand Beach County Park, Skanee, for salmon and trout.

Culture and Entertainment

Chapter 8

Museums

Museums take many shapes and forms in Michigan, from internationally renowned collections to tiny, community-based operations housed in a single room. Together, they display, illuminate, preserve, and interpret our heritage and technologies, both human and natural. Many provide research facilities with books, maps, and other documents for the casual reader and serious scholar.

The listings here are limited to those with free admission, although most welcome voluntary contributions. Others, including several historical museums run by the Secretary of State, are omitted although their own admission is free because there is a charge to enter the state parks in which they are located. Also omitted are museums that require a donation, even if the amount of the contribution is left to each visitor's discretion, and those that limit free admission to school groups or senior citizens. Included, however, are museums that do not charge admission on certain regularly scheduled days but collect a fee at other times.

The listings indicate whether classes, programs, tours, and reference facilities also are free. Some request an appointment or prior arrangements to use their research material.

Before you visit, verify hours due to holidays, festivals, special happenings, or renovations. For instance, schedules for college-affiliated museums sometimes change to reflect vacations, semester breaks, and major campus events. Budgetary factors such as grants and government support, as well as the availability of volunteers, also affect operating hours.

Codes are Y (yes) and N (no) for tours, programs/lectures, classes, and reference library.

SOUTHEAST

Jackson County

Dewey School Museum (517) 851-8247   Y N N Y
11501 Territorial Road June–August
Stockbridge MI 49285 Sunday, 1–4
 September weekends, 1–4

This is a refurbished, one-room brick pioneer school equipped to teach with hands-on artifacts. The grassy school yard appears as it did in the late 1800s and early 1900s.

Mann House (517) 524-8943   Y Y N N
205 Hanover Mid-May–mid-October
Concord MI 49237 Thurs.–Sun., 1–5

This state-run museum is located in a three-story 1884 house built by local farmers Daniel and Ellen Mann. The building interprets the Victorian era through artifacts, architecture, and landscaping, including furniture, books, decorative arts, and toys. The carriage barn and Victorian gardens also are open to visitors. The museum hosts an annual Victorian Music Fest.

Lapeer County

Imlay City Historical Museum (313) 724-1111   Y Y Y Y
77 Main St. April–December
Imlay City MI 48444 Weekends, 1:30–4:30

Local history is featured.

Lenawee County

Hudson Museum (517) 448-8858   Y Y N Y
219 W. Main St. Year-round
Hudson MI 49247 Mon., Wed., and Fri.,
  1–4:30
 Saturday, Noon–3

Housed in an 1867 former bank building, the collection includes weapons and other military items from the Civil War, World War I, and World War II, memorabilia from early merchants and manufacturers, pioneer and Victorian clothing, and artifacts of everyday life. There's an early physician's office with instruments and furnishings.

Lenawee County Historical Museum
110 E. Church St.
Box 511
Adrian MI 49221

(517) 265-6071   Y N N Y
Year-round
Tues.–Sat., 1–5

Exhibits focus on the county's settlement and development and include a dugout canoe, arrowheads, early farm implements, and pioneer furniture, toys, and dolls. There are artifacts from the Erie and Kalamazoo Railroad, the nation's first railroad west of the Hudson River, and possessions of Laura Haviland, an Adrian Quaker abolitionist, feminist, and educator of the late 1800s. An early twentieth-century Murray automobile, locally built, is on display with business and political memorabilia. Archives include business, education, government, and genealogical records, plus personal letters, maps, and photos. The castlelike Romanesque building is on the National Register of Historic Places.

Walker Tavern Historic Complex
13220 M-50
Brooklyn MI 48230

(517) 467-4414   Y Y N N
Memorial Day–mid-September
Daily, 10–5

This 1840s Federal-style white clapboard house became a stagecoach stop along the Detroit-Chicago Road in the Irish Hills region. In addition to the original house with its period furniture, there are a reconstructed barn of the same era, Michigan Bicentennial wagon, and a visitor center. Exhibits, audiovisual presentations, and walking tours present the history of Michigan's stagecoach era. The annual summertime Toledo War Days commemorate the virtually bloodless 1835 "war" between the state of Ohio and Michigan Territory with militia encampments, nineteenth-century craft demonstrations, and other events.

Macomb County

Michigan Transit Museum (313) 463-1863 Y N N N
Cass Avenue Year-round
Mt. Clemens MI Weekends, 1–4
Mailing Address: Box 12
Fraser MI 48026

Exhibits include turn-of-the-century railroad and electric traction artifacts. The museum is in a restored, 1859 brick depot built by the Grand Trunk Railway as part of its main line between eastern Canada and Chicago. It was here that a young Thomas Edison learned telegraphy.

Romeo Historical Museum (313) 752-4111 Y N N N
132 Church St. Year-round
Romeo MI 48065 Saturday, 1–4

The museum offers an extensive collection of local artifacts, including paintings by nineteenth-century Romeo artist William Gibbs, historic clothing, documents, and furniture. Displays change seasonally.

Selfridge Military Air Museum (313) 466-5035 N N N Y
Selfridge Air National Guard Base April 1–Oct. 31
Mt. Clemens MI 48045 Sunday, 1–5

Military aircraft on display include fighters, cargo craft, bombers, a jet trainer, reconnaissance and antisubmarine patrol planes, and a helicopter. Indoor exhibits include aircraft engines, military aviation artifacts, scale models of aircraft, historic photos of the base and its units, and aircraft drawings and paintings.

Monroe County

Monroe County Historical Museum (313) 243-7137 N N N Y
126 S. Monroe St. May 1–Sept. 30
Monroe MI 48161 Tues.–Sun., 10–5
  Oct. 1–April 30
  Wed.–Sun., 10–5

Located on the site of George Armstrong Custer's home, the museum contains a large collection of eighteenth- and nineteenth-century southeast Michigan artifacts and examples of Victorian furniture, clothing, and decorative arts. Exhibits trace the lives of Custer, who moved to Monroe at age 10, and his widow, Elizabeth Bacon. Other exhibits focus on early native Americans of the region, French settlers, and Michigan history leading up to 1837 statehood and beyond.

Old Mill Museum		Y Y N N
242 Toledo St.	Memorial Day–Labor Day	
Dundee MI 48131	Weekends, 1–4	

Among the exhibits are a time line depicting local scenes, including the early years of the old mill, its reconstruction by Henry Ford, enlarged pictures from that project, as well as a street and store facade.

River Raisin Battlefield Visitor Center	(313) 243-7136	Y Y N N
1403 E. Elm Ave.	May–September	
Monroe MI 48161	Daily, 9–5	
	October–April	
	Weekends, 9–5	

Exhibits explain the 1813 Battle of River Raisin and the War of 1812 in the old Northwest Territory, which included Michigan. A 14-minute audiovisual presentation describes the battle, one of the largest of that war.

Oakland County

Birmingham Bloomfield Art Association	(313) 644-0866	N N N Y
1516 S. Cranbrook Road	Year-round	
Birmingham MI 48009	Mon.–Sat., 9:30–4:30	

This is a community art center with changing exhibits. An average of nine exhibitions are put on each year. Shows include the works of students and faculty, with at least one major regional or national show annually.

Clawson Historical Museum   (313) 588-9169   Y Y N Y
41 Fisher Court   Year-round
Clawson MI 48017   Wed. and Sun., 1–4

The museum is located in a house built by Oswald and Deborah Fisher in about 1920, the year the village was incorporated. Furnishings, toys, appliances, and other articles are typical of the 1920s, including a 1928 player piano that visitors can use. There are also artifacts and memorabilia from earlier in local history. More than 100 photos depicting Clawson's history are displayed in the Community Room.

Holocaust Memorial Center   (313) 661-0840   Y Y N Y
6602 W. Maple Road   Year-round
W. Bloomfield MI 48322   Sun.–Thurs., 10–3:30

Opened in 1984, the center was set up to document the history of the European Jewish community and its virtual destruction in the Holocaust of World War II. There are photographs, a video presentation of the testimony of Holocaust survivors, cartoons from Nazi newspapers, audio-visual displays, and a memorial flame for the 6 million Jewish victims of Nazism. An extensive research library includes books, microfilmed documents, and oral histories.

Milford Historical Museum   (313) 685-7308   Y N N Y
124 E. Commerce St.   March–mid-December
Milford MI 48381   Wed. and Sat., 1–4

Since its construction in 1853, this Greek Revival house built by John Wood served as a home and government offices before it became a museum. One floor is furnished in late Victorian era style, with a formal parlor, kitchen, bedroom, toy room, and dining room. Special exhibits appear on the first floor, covering such themes as one-room schools, Saturday night baths, and prestatehood log cabins.

Northeast Oakland Historical   (313) 628-3519   Y Y N Y
  Museum   Year-round
1 N. Washington St.   Saturday, 1–4
Oxford MI 48371   June–August
                                             Wed. and Sat., 1–4

The museum is located in a 1922 bank building. It features 1880s furniture and clothing, antique quilts, a tin shop, Victorian kitchen and dining room, old kitchen and housekeeping items, small farm and carpenter tools, an Edison phonograph, old typewriter collection, and WPA murals of Oxford.

Creative Arts Center (313) 333-7849 Y N N Y
47 Williams St. Year-round
Pontiac MI 48341 Tues., Wed., Thurs., and
Sat., 10–4

Changing arts exhibits.

Troy Museum and Historic Village (313) 524-3570 N N N Y
60 W. Wattles Road Year-round
Troy MI 48098 Tues.–Sat., 9–5:30
Sunday, 1–5

The museum is in the former township and city hall. The main 1927 building is modeled after a Dutch colonial tavern in Troy, New York. Other buildings include an 1820s log cabin, 1832 Greek Revival house, 1900 print shop, 1875 wagon shop, 1877 school, and a replica of an 1832 general store. The museum also features such seasonal events as Heritage Day, Summer Sights and Sounds, Harvest Home Festival, and Hanging of the Greens.

St. Clair County

Knowlton's Ice Museum (313) 987-7100 Y Y N N
1755 Yeager St. May–October
Port Huron MI 48060 By appointment

This museum boasts the country's largest collection of ice-harvesting tools and related items. More than 1,000 artifacts are in the collection, including ice boxes, tools, and an antique ice wagon. A rare early 1920s film of ice harvesting in Wisconsin is shown.

Museum of Arts and History (313) 982-0891   N N N N
1115 6th St. Year-round
Port Huron MI 48060 Wed.–Sun., 1–4:30

A gallery of marine lore includes artifacts, ship models, and a reconstructed Great Lakes freighter pilothouse. Among the other exhibits are mammoth bones, archeological remains of a Woodlands Culture fishing village, scenes of the seventeenth-century French-built Fort St. Joseph and the nineteenth-century American-built Fort Gratiot, railroad models, and memorabilia from inventor Thomas Alva Edison's local boyhood home.

Pride and Heritage Museum (313) 765-5446   Y N N Y
405 S. Main St. April–December
Box 184 Weekends, 1–4
Marine City MI 48039

The museum features artifacts relating to the city's shipbuilding heritage, including ship models, paintings, and items retrieved by divers in the St. Clair River. Also on display are World War I memorabilia, items from the defunct Mariner Theater, a blacksmith shop, and old farm equipment and tools. The building, originally home to Newport Academy and later a library and jail, is a state historic site.

St. Clair Historical Museum (313) 329-6888   Y N N Y
308 S. Fourth St. April–December
St. Clair MI 48079 Weekends, 1:30–4:30

Housed in the former First Baptist Church, displays include gowns, tools, toys, pictures, and other artifacts of early St. Clair history. The building is a state historic site.

Washtenaw County

Kelsey Museum of Archaeology (313) 764-9304   N   Y   N   Y
434 S. State St. Year-round
Ann Arbor MI 48109 Labor Day–May 1
 Mon.–Fri., 9–4
 Weekends, 1–4
 May 1–Labor Day
 Tues.–Fri., 11–4
 Weekends, 1–4

The museum, on the University of Michigan campus, contains nearly 100,000 artifacts from ancient and early medieval cultures of the Near East, Greece, Rome, and Egypt. Highlights include textiles, pottery, coins, sculpture, and glass, plus an array of items reflecting daily life in Roman Egypt.

Stearns Collection of (313) 763-4389   N   Y   N   Y
  Musical Instruments Year-round
School of Music Thurs.–Fri., 10–5
University of Michigan Weekends, 1–6
Ann Arbor MI 48109

The museum displays part of a permanent collection of more than 2,000 instruments, some fanciful and some historically significant, from around the world, including electronic instruments. There are galleries, hands-on exhibits, and a three-dimensional hologram machine.

University of Michigan (313) 764-0395   Y   Y   Y   Y
  Museum of Art Year-round
525 S. State St. Tues.–Sat., 10–5
Ann Arbor MI 48109 Sunday, 1–5

This is a rich permanent collection from Western and Asian traditions. Of particular note are Chinese and Japanese paintings, Old Master and contemporary prints, and more than 100 etchings and lithographs by J. M. Whistler. In addition to its permanent collection, there are special exhibitions, family programs, concerts, films, and interpretive programs.

Wayne County

Canton Township Historical Museum 1150 S. Canton Center Road Canton MI 48188	(313) 397-0088 March–December Tuesday, 1–3 Saturday, 1–4	Y Y N Y

The collection highlights rural heritage with farm implements, clothing, family histories, and school information. It's in a restored, 1884 one-room schoolhouse.

Children's Museum of the Detroit Public Schools 67 E. Kirby Detroit MI 48202	(313) 494-1210 Year-round Mon.–Fri., 1–4 Weekends, 9–4 Closed summer weekends	N Y N Y

The museum, a major resource for local schools, also provides exhibits and activities, including a planetarium and changing exhibits about multicultural heritage, dinosaurs, folk arts, and other subjects. Habitat groups and extinct passenger pigeons are permanently displayed in the Bird Room. Children can climb on the front lawn sculpture, Silverbolt, a horse fashioned from auto bumpers.

Moross House 1460 E. Jefferson Detroit MI 48207	(313) 259-6363 Year-round Tues.–Thurs., 9:30–3:30	N N N Y

Moross House was built in Modified Greek Revival style in 1843–48 and is the city's oldest surviving brick house. Now restored, the front hallway and parlor were furnished by the Detroit Historical Museum with period antiques. It serves as headquarters for the Detroit Garden Center, a non-profit organization dedicated to horticultural education; inside it boasts the state's most complete horticultural library.

Children's Museum. (Courtesy Detroit Public Schools.)

Dossin Great Lakes Museum (313) 267-6440 N N N Y
100 Strand Drive Year-round
Belle Isle Wed.–Sun., 10–4
Detroit MI 48207

This municipal museum on the Detroit River houses an outstanding collection about the Great Lakes and the boats that sailed them. Exhibits include a restored pilothouse from the freighter *William Clay Ford*, the restored 40-foot hydroplane *Miss Pepsi*, and the Gothic Room lounge from the 1912 D & C passenger steamer *City of Detroit III*, the world's largest sidewheeler when it was launched in 1912. It has scale models of Great Lakes ships from canoes to lakers, and such special exhibits as one about the Storm of November 8, 1913, the most destructive storm to hit the Great Lakes since commercial navigation began; eight freighters were lost without survivors on Lake Huron alone.

Grosse Ile Historical Society Parkway and East River Box 131 Grosse Ile MI 48138	April–December Thursday, 10–Noon Sunday, 1–4	N Y N Y

The museum occupies two buildings, a 1906 Michigan Central Railroad depot and an 1871 U.S. Customs House. They hold artifacts, clothing, furniture, photos, and archives relating to the history of Grosse Ile.

Museum of African-American History 301 Frederick Douglass Detroit MI 48202	(313) 833-9800 Year-round Wed.–Sat., 9:30–5 Sunday, 1–4	Y Y Y Y

There are special guided tours of the permanent exhibition, "Epic of Freedom: The Underground Railroad in Michigan," and an annual celebration of the African holiday of Kwanza.

Pewabic Pottery 10125 E. Jefferson Ave. Detroit MI 48214	(313) 822-0954 Year-round Tues.–Sat., 10–6	N Y N Y

Housed in a historic 1906–7 building, the museum includes original clay machinery, the Pewabic Pottery ceramic collection, a contemporary ceramic gallery, and furniture of the Arts and Crafts Movement.

Trenton Historical Museum 306 St. Joseph Ave. Trenton MI 48183	(313) 675-2130 February–July Saturday, 1–4	Y N N N

Located in the renovated home of tavernkeepers John and Sarah Moore, the museum is furnished with Victorian artifacts and furniture. It features Trenton's first post office and a carriage house with a large church bell.

SOUTHWEST

Berrien County

Fort Miami Heritage Society (616) 983-1191   N Y N Y
708 Market St. Year-round
St. Joseph MI 49085 Monday, 1–5
 Tues.–Wed., 9–Noon
 Thursday, 9–5
 Friday, 9–4

The museum focuses on local history. Located in an 1859 Congregational church building, it's now called the Landmark Center.

Krasl Art Center (616) 983-0271   Y Y N Y
707 Lake Blvd. Year-round
St. Joseph MI 49085 Mon.–Thurs. and Sat., 10–4
 Friday, 10–1
 Sunday, 1–4

The museum features three galleries with exhibits that change monthly. It also hosts the annual All-Michigan All-Media Competition and sponsors an annual art fair.

Siegfried H. Horn (616) 471-3273   Y Y Y N
 Archaeological Museum Year-round
Andrews University Tues.–Thurs., 9–Noon
Berrien Springs MI 49104 and 2–5
 Weekends, 2–5

The collection consists of archaeological objects from the Near East, dating from the Stone Age through the Islamic Period. They include ceramic and glass objects, figurines, jewelry, inscriptions, seals, seal impressions, and weapons from Palestine, Syria, Egypt, and Mesopotamia, as well as a replica of the Rosetta Stone. There are also two significant specialized collections: 3,000 cuneiform tablets and 900 coins. Among the items of particular interest are a rare Syrian statue of Baal, a sixth-century B.C. Babylonian brick with the stamp of Nebuchadnezzar, and two Roman period wooden statues covered with gold leaf.

Calhoun County

Art Center of Battle Creek 265 E. Emmett St. Battle Creek MI 49017	(616) 962-9511 Sept. 1–July 1 Tues.–Fri., 10–5 Weekends, 1–4	N	N	N	N

The museum offers changing art exhibitions, many of which highlight the work of Michigan artists and artisans. Some exhibitions feature hands-on activities for children.

Blair Historical Farm 24655 M-60 East Homer MI 49245	(517) 568-3116 June–September By appointment	Y	N	N	N

Much of the furniture on display belonged to the family that built this farmhouse in 1875. The sitting room table was built from walnut trees grown on the farm. Other artifacts include household items and farm tools.

Brueckner Museum and Gladsome Cottage Museum 13725 26 Mile Road Starr Commonwealth Road Albion MI 49224	(517) 629-5591 Year-round Mon.–Fri., 8:30–4:30	Y	N	N	N

These two museums are on the grounds of the Starr Commonwealth Schools, a nationally renowned facility for troubled youth. Gladsome Cottage contains Victorian furniture, paintings, and artifacts from the United States, Europe, and Asia. The white frame cottage was built in 1913 and became the first electrified rural home in Calhoun County. Brueckner Museum features paintings, drawings, prints, sculptures, and stained glass windows. The 350-acre campus is a state historic site, and a walking tour map is available.

Gardner House Museum (517) 629-5402 Y Y N Y
509 S. Superior St. April–October
Albion MI 49224 Weekends, 1–4

The museum is in a brick house built by hardware merchant Augustus P. Gardner in 1875 and refurbished for museum use. Furnished in Victorian style, it represents a typical house of the late nineteenth century, with artifacts and furniture that once belonged to area homes. There are local history displays as well as a representation of a typical 1900-era neighborhood store. Research facilities include genealogical and photo archives. It's on the National Register of Historic Places.

Cass County

Pioneer Log Cabin Museum (616) 445-2965 N N N N
South Broadway Memorial Day–Labor
Cassopolis MI 49031 Day Weekend
Thurs.–Sun., Noon–5

Exhibits focus on natural and local history. Among them are a collection of stuffed birds and animals, including a passenger pigeon. The museum is housed in a log cabin built in 1923 on the shore of Stone Lake. There is a Log Cabin festival held here each June featuring such pioneer crafts as butter churning.

Kalamazoo County

Alamo Township Museum (616) 344-7559 N Y Y Y
8119 N. 6th St. or 344-9579
Kalamazoo MI 49009 April–November
Tuesday, 9–11
Weekends, 2–4

The main part of the museum is in the township's oldest building, originally an 1865 Presbyterian Church. Its displays include pioneer pictures, antique office machines, cobbler's tools, a children's section, and a Victorian kitchen, bedroom, and parlor. The Alamo Farm Barn contains artifacts and displays highlighting blacksmithing, Michigan railroad history, and 200 years of farming.

Kalamazoo Institute of Arts (616) 349-7775 Y Y Y Y
314 S. Park St. Sept. 1–July 31
Kalamazoo MI 49007 Tues.–Sat., 10–5
 Sunday, 1–5

The museum's collection of twentieth-century contemporary art includes paintings, ceramics, prints, photographs, and sculpture. Some sculptures are located in outdoor courtyards. It hosts more than 30 exhibits a year from its own collection or on loan from other institutions and private collectors, as well as a juried area show and a large annual art fair.

Ottawa County

Holland Area Arts Council (616) 396-3278 Y Y N N
25 W. 8th St. Year-round
Holland MI 49423 Monday, Noon–9
 Tues.–Fri., 10–9
 Saturday, 9–4
 Sunday, 2–5

The council hosts monthly exhibits of Michigan artists, student shows, competitions, and touring exhibitions. It also presents free workshops.

Van Buren County

Liberty Hyde Bailey Museum (616) 637-3251 Y Y Y Y
903 Bailey Ave. Year-round
South Haven MI 49090 Tues. and Fri., 2–4:30

This white frame house was the birthplace of Liberty Hyde Bailey, one of the nation's most influential horticulturists and botanists. Its bedrooms are furnished in period style. Visitors can see furniture, books, and other items used by the Bailey family, as well as nineteenth-century household furnishings, clothing, toys, quilts, and pictures. Also displayed are collections of arrowheads, tools, rocks, knives, and medicine bottles.

CENTRAL

Bay County

Historical Museum of Bay County 321 Washington Ave. Bay City MI 48708	(517) 893-5733 Year-round Mon.–Fri., 10–5 Sunday, 1–5	N	Y	N	Y

The museum has more than 60,000 locally significant historic artifacts as well as changing exhibits, an extensive research library, and special programs.

Eaton County

Bellevue Memorial Museum 212 N. Main St. Bellevue MI 49021	(616) 763-3369 Year-round Mon.–Fri., 1–6	N	N	N	Y

Bellevue was the first settlement in Eaton County, and the museum displays a small collection of local historic artifacts. It's attached to the public library.

Museum of the Grand Ledge Area
   Historical Society
118 W. Lincoln
Box 203
Grand Ledge MI 48837
	(517) 627-3149 or
	  627-5170
	Year-round
	Sunday, 2–4
		N	Y	N	Y

This local history museum is housed in an 1880 Gothic Revival House. Local theme exhibits change twice a year.

Vermontville Museum 109 N. Main Vermontville MI 49096	(517) 726-0518 Spring–Fall Variable hours and by appointment	Y	N	Y	Y

The museum, which features local history, was built as an academy and church in 1843.

Genesee County

Chester H. Wilson Geology Museum
1401 E. Court St.
Gorman Building, Room 339–41
Flint MI 48503

(313) 232-6291   Y Y N N
Year-round
Mon.–Fri., 8–3

Located on the Mott Community College campus, the museum features rocks, minerals, and fossils from around the world. Among its special displays are collections of Michigan minerals and fossils, miniature minerals, and minerals of Mexico, South America, and Africa. Collectors frequently donate new specimens.

Grand Blanc Heritage Museum
203 E. Grand Blanc Road
Grand Blanc MI 48439

(313) 694-7274   Y Y Y Y
September–November and
January–June
Wednesday, 10–2

The 1885 building contains memorabilia about the township's schools, businesses, buildings, and residents. There's a school room, a tool room, and such artifacts as a cider press, treadle sewing machines, Victrola, arrowheads, peace pipe, old toys, and wooden washing machine. There are also temporary displays from private collections. Once a Congregational church and later used for municipal offices, it's a state historic site.

Gratiot County

Gratiot County Area Historical Museum
129 W. Center
Ithaca MI 48847

(517) 875-4974   Y Y N Y
Mid-May–mid-December
Wednesday, 10–2

The museum hosts changing exhibits on the history of the area and features a Victorian parlor display and Letter Carrier's Room.

Ingham County

Telephone Pioneer Museum (517) 372-1400   N N N N
221 N. Washington Square Year-round
Lansing MI 48933 Tues. and Fri., 10–2

Located in the Michigan Bell building, the museum includes artifacts, equipment, and photographs about the history of telephone service such as hand-cranked phones, 1930s poles, antique switchboards, and computers.

Kresge Art Museum (517) 355-7631   Y Y N Y
Auditorium Road or 353-9834
Michigan State University Year-round
East Lansing MI 48824 Mon.–Wed. and Fri., 9:30–4:30
Thursday, Noon–8
Weekends, 1–4

Founded in 1959, the museum is home to MSU's permanent collection of more than 4,000 works of art, from prehistoric to contemporary. The museum hosts frequent special exhibitions on art history and shows the works of international artists, MSU faculty, and MSU students.

Michigan Historical Museum (517) 373-3559   Y Y Y Y
717 W. Allegan St. Year-round
Lansing MI 48918 Mon.–Fri., 9–4:30
Saturday, 10–4
Sunday, 1–5

This stellar museum a few blocks from the Capitol takes visitors through Michigan's geological, political, social, cultural, mining, agricultural, and industrial past, from prehistory through the twentieth century. Among the major exhibits are a walk-through Upper Peninsula copper mine, lumber baron's mansion, and life-sized woodland fur-trading diorama. The museum also offers audiovisual presentations, temporary exhibits, special programs, and entertainment. Extensive research facilities are found in the adjacent State Archives and State Library.

Michigan State University　　(517) 355-2370　　Y　Y　Y　Y
　Museum　　　　　　　　　　Year-round
East Lansing MI 48824　　　　Mon.–Wed., 9–5
　　　　　　　　　　　　　　Thursday, 9–9
　　　　　　　　　　　　　　Saturday, 10–5
　　　　　　　　　　　　　　Sunday, 1–5

The collection's specialties are natural and cultural history, combining permanent and special exhibits. Among the most popular are stegosaurus, allosaurus, and African elephant skeletons, wildlife dioramas, bird and mammal specimens, fossils, and displays about native American and world cultures, crafts, and traditional arts. The museum is a center for research in Michigan folklife, archaeology, agricultural history, and vertebrate paleontology and biology.

Kresge Art Museum. (Courtesy Michigan State University.)

Isabella County

Center for Cultural and Natural History 124 Rowe Hall Central Michigan University Mt. Pleasant MI 48859	(517) 774-3829 Year-round Mon.–Fri., 8–5 September–April Weekends, 1–4	Y Y N N

There are artifacts and exhibits about anthropology, geology, mammalogy, ornithology, herpetology, ichthyology, and ornithology. Among them are fossils, prehistoric Michigan Indian pots, and a 420-pound Petoskey stone, the largest ever found in the state. There also are Civil War weapons, Victorian toys, skeletal remains of a mastodon, handmade tools, and a live display of poisonous snakes.

Shepherd Historical Society Museum and Little Red Schoolhouse Museum 314 W. Maple St. Box 505 Shepherd MI 48883	 March–December 2d Monday night of each month, 7:30–10 and by appointment	Y N N Y

The museum is representative of the community, with a general room, historic kitchen, living-dining room and bedroom, and a section depicting early 1900s stores. It's open when the historical society holds its monthly meeting, during the annual Maple Syrup Festival the last weekend of April, and by appointment.

University Art Gallery Franklin and Preston Mt. Pleasant MI 48859	(517) 774-3800 Sept. 1–mid-July Mon.–Fri., 10–5 Saturday, 10–4	Y Y N N

The museum on the Central Michigan University campus features media exhibitions and student shows.

Livingston County

Gage House 6440 Kensington Road Box 84 Brighton MI 48116	(313) 437-1271 June–Labor Day Weekends, 1–4	Y	N	N	N

The museum, located in a centennial farmhouse, has 12 rooms of artifacts including a Civil War collection, native American items, and maps. There are sewing, nature, milk, wash, and children's rooms, as well as a kitchen and pantry.

Midland County

Automotive Hall of Fame 3225 Cook Road Box 1727 Midland MI 48641-1727	(517) 631-5760 Year-round Mon.–Fri., 9–4	Y	N	N	Y

Located on the campus of Northwood Institute, the museum displays memorabilia and plaques that honor major contributors to the auto industry.

Midland Art Council 1801 W. St. Andrews St. Midland MI 48640	(517) 631-3250 Year-round Mon.–Fri., 10–5 Weekends, 1–5	Y	N	N	N

Changing exhibits.

Midland County Historical Society 1801 W. St. Andrews St. Midland MI 48640	(517) 835-7401 Year-round Mon.–Fri., 10–6 Weekends, 1–5	N	N	N	Y

Located in the Midland Center for the Arts, the museum features historical exhibits about early Midland family life, fashions, architecture, and crafts. Some exhibits are from its own collection, while others are on loan.

Saginaw County

Historical Society of Bridgeport (517) 777-5230 Y Y Y Y
6190 Dixie Highway Year-round
Box 337 Tuesday, 1–4
Bridgeport MI 48722 Thursday, 1–4 and 7–9

Local history, with lectures and classes in the Little Red School.

Marshall M. Fredericks (517) 790-5667 Y Y N Y
  Sculpture Gallery Year-round
Saginaw Valley State University Tues.–Sun., 1–5
University Center MI 48710

More than 200 works by internationally renowned sculptor Marshall M. Fredericks are housed here. There are original models for many of his greatest pieces, including *Spirit of Detroit* (Detroit,) *Expanding Universe Fountain* (Washington), and *Freedom of the Human Spirit* (New York City). Also shown are sketches, portraits, and drawings, as well as photos of Fredericks at work. An adjacent garden holds more than a dozen bronze casts.

Saginaw Art Museum (517) 754-2491 Y Y N N
1126 N. Michigan Ave. Year-round
Saginaw MI 48602 Tues.–Sat., 10–5
  Sunday, 1–5

The permanent collection includes more than 700 objects ranging from ancient Near Eastern pottery to Asian art and contemporary American prints and paintings, with an emphasis on nineteenth- and twentieth-century American art. There is a special collection of works by E. Irving Couse, a Saginaw native. More than 30 exhibitions are held annually, featuring historic and contemporary works in a variety of styles and media from around the world. "Visionarea" is a special gallery with participatory activities for children. The museum is housed in a 1904 Georgian Revival building with formal gardens and is on the National Register of Historic Places.

Saginaw Railway Museum (517) 792-9360   Y Y N N
900 Maple St.   May–November
Saginaw MI 48602   Weekends, 10–3

The museum preserves and displays artifacts and information important to American railroad history. The museum's main building is a 1907 depot. Also on the site are an 1898 interlocking tower, maintenance shed with tools of the trade, and a boxcar, kitchen car, and two cabooses.

Shiawassee County

Michigan Railroad History   (517) 288-3561   Y Y N Y
  Museum   Year-round
200 Railroad St.   Mon.–Fri., 9–5
Box 106   Saturday, 1–5
Durand MI 48429   Sunday (May–Oct.), 1–5

Union Station is one of the nation's largest remaining small town stations. A story line at the state's official railroad history museum tells how railroads developed in Michigan. There's also a working HO-scale train and trolley diorama. A former Grand Trunk Western steam locomotive is located nearby, as is a former baggage car being used as a local railroad history museum.

NORTHEAST

Alpena County

Jesse Besser Museum   (517) 356-2202   N Y N Y
491 Johnson St.   Year-round
Alpena MI 49707   Monday, 2–5
                      Friday, 10–5

This museum is free only during the listed hours; admission is charged at other times. It covers science, art, and regional history, including exhibits on agriculture and lumbering. Also on the grounds are restored nineteenth-century buildings, including a one-room schoolhouse, a bank, and a homesteader's cabin. Special exhibits of art, crafts, photography, and other subjects are presented throughout the year.

Arenac County

Arenac County Historical Museum (517) 876-8757 or   Y Y Y Y
304 E. Michigan Ave.   876-6399
Box 272   May–November
AuGres MI 48703   Weekends, 1–5

Originally an 1883 country Gothic church, the museum now offers both permanent and temporary exhibits. Among them are a rural school room, pioneer kitchen, vintage clothing, bedroom and parlor settings, quilts, and a barber and apothecary shop. The collection also includes farming, agricultural, commercial fishing, and native American artifacts, shipbuilding tools, and a scale model diorama of the highest wooden railroad bridge built in the state.

Cheboygan County

Mackinac Bridge Museum   (616) 436-5276   N N N N
231 Central Ave.   April–October
Box 148   Daily, 8–Noon
Mackinaw City MI 49701

The museum features original tools and materials used to build the five-mile Mackinac Bridge, the world's longest suspension bridge. A film about construction of the bridge is also shown.

Huron County

Frank Murphy Museum   (517) 479-6310   N N N N
Main Street   June–September
Harbor Beach MI 48441   Daily, 9–5

The museum is dedicated to Harbor Beach native Frank Murphy, who was mayor of Detroit, U.S. governor-general of the Philippines, governor of Michigan, U.S. attorney general, and ultimately a U.S. Supreme Court justice. It contains his papers and artifacts from his life.

Pigeon Historical Depot Museum (517) 453-3242 Y N N N
59 S. Main St. June–Sept. 1
Pigeon MI 48755 Saturday, 10–1
Sunday, 2–4

The museum is housed in a restored, century-old railroad depot. It's been designated a state historic site.

Pioneer Log Village (517) 269-8165 Y Y N N
223 Willis St. May 15–Oct. 15
Bad Axe MI 48413 Sunday, 2–5

Six log buildings constructed between 1872 and 1895 have been moved from elsewhere in Huron County to Bad Axe City Park: a home, school, chapel, general store, barn, and blacksmith shop. Each is restored and features appropriate exhibits. An annual Log Cabin Day celebration includes music, extended tour hours, and pioneer craft demonstrations.

Lighthouse Park Museum (517) 428-4749 Y N N N
7320 Lighthouse Road May 30–Oct. 1
Port Hope MI 48468 Weekends, Noon–4

The museum features shipwreck artifacts and photographs.

Presque Isle County

Presque Isle County (517) 734-4121 Y N N Y
  Historical Museum Mid-May–mid-October
176 W. Michigan Mon.–Fri., Noon–4
Box 175 May–June
Rogers City MI 49779 Weekends, Noon–4
July–August
Saturday, Noon–4

Formerly the home of Calcite president Carl D. Bradley, the museum includes native American artifacts, an 1890s general store, Victorian music room, and displays about lumbering, fishing, and shipping in Presque Isle County.

Roscommon County

Houghton Lake Area Historical (517) 366-9124   Y N N N
  Society Village   June 1–Labor Day
1701 W. Houghton Lake Drive   Wed.–Fri., 10–4
Box 14   Weekends, 10–6
Houghton Lake MI 48629

The buildings include a print shop, doctor's office, blacksmith shop, homestead, pharmacy, chapel, and carriage shop, with a museum in the log schoolhouse. There also are a nature trail and band shell. Special events include a historical roundup and Christmas lighting of the village.

NORTHWEST

Antrim County

Bellaire Area Historical Museum   (616) 533-8943 or   N N N Y
Community Building   533-8631
Box 646   June 1–Sept. 1
Bellaire MI 49615   Mon.–Fri., 11–3

Displayed here are the keepsakes and collections of local residents covering 1865–1965. They include pictures of lumbering days, clothing, tools, school items, toys, newspapers, and artifacts from local businesses and manufacturers.

Elk Rapids Museum   (616) 264-9333 or   N Y N Y
401 Spruce St.   264-8886
Elk Rapids MI 49629   June–September
                          Tues.–Sun., 1–4
                          Fall–Winter
                          Weekends, 1–4

Housed in the lower level of the Elk Rapids Township Hall, the museum presents artifacts and information on the area's lumbering era, Elk Rapids Iron Co., and the boats that traveled the Chain of Lakes years ago. There's a large antique piano on display, along with a replica of the Iron Works, a bust of Antrim County pioneer settler Abram Wadsworth, and a large split tree with rings marked to denote local, national, and world events. The building, finished in 1883, was known as the Grand Opera House and is on the National Register of Historic Places.

Charlevoix County

East Jordan Portside Art and   (616) 536-2393   Y   Y   N   Y
   Historical Museum   June–October
Elm Pointe Estate   Wed.–Sun., 1–4
M-66 South
East Jordan MI 49727

The museum contains lumbering and agricultural exhibits, turn-of-the-century clothing, opera house memorabilia, photos, and a collection of industrial records.

Grand Traverse County

Schooner *Madeline*   (616) 946-2647   Y   Y   Y   Y
Clinch Park Marina   May–October
Box 1108   Mon.–Fri., 10–6
Traverse City MI 49685   Weekends, Noon–6

This 56-foot replica of the 1845 Great Lakes working schooner *Madeline* is docked at the marina in Traverse City. As a floating museum, it offers exhibits about the ship's history and the relationship between maritime history and people's everyday life.

Walter E. Hastings Museum   (616) 276-9221   Y   Y   N   N
Interlochen Arts Camp   Summer
Box 199   Tues.–Sat., 8–6
Interlochen MI 49643   Sunday, 1–5:30

The museum, located at the Interlochen Arts Camp, includes collections of arrowheads, polished and rough stones, Indian and Eskimo artifacts, sea shells, and fluorescent rocks.

Kalkaska County

Kalkaska County Historical Museum　(616) 258-8285　Y　N　N　Y
Cedar Street　　　　　　　　　　　　June–August
Box 216　　　　　　　　　　　　　　 Mon.–Sat., 1–4
Kalkaska MI 49646

The museum features memorabilia of pioneering days in Kalkaska County. On display are a homemade cedar smokehouse, handmade 1898 car, 1929 Durant car, locally manufactured products, and other items. It's located in an old railroad depot building, built in 1911 to replace one that had burned down. The research library contains information about local families, government, industries, businesses, clubs, and fraternal organizations.

Leelanau County

Sleeping Bear Point Coast　　　(616) 326-5134　N　Y　N　Y
　Guard Station　　　　　　　　Spring–Fall
Sleeping Bear Dunes　　　　　　Daily, 9–4
　National Lakeshore
Box 277
Empire MI 49630

Housed in a restored former Coast Guard station in Glen Haven, it features exhibits and photos about shipwrecks, Great Lakes shipping, the history of the U.S. Life Saving Service—the forerunner of today's Coast Guard—and the Coast Guard itself. The station, similar to about five dozen along the Great Lakes, was built in 1901; in 1931, it was moved a half-mile because drifting sand threatened the buildings, and heavy surf made it difficult to launch rescue boats. The museum has a restored surfmen's bunkroom and lake steamer pilot house exhibit. The boathouse represents the Life Saving era of 1901–15 with lifeboat, surfboat, line-throwing gun, beach car, and safety gear and apparatus. A video presentation shows a beach apparatus drill, and you can listen to a taped interview with a retired Coast Guard commandant who grew up in this station and the lifesaving stations on North and South Manitou islands. The museum is operated by the National Park Service and is north of the park's visitor center (for more information on the park, see chap. 1).

Muskegon County

Montague Museum Church Street Montague MI 49437	Memorial Day–Labor Day Weekends, 1–5	Y	Y	N	Y

The museum focuses on local history and has an extensive collection of historic photos.

Muskegon County Museum 430 W. Clay Ave. Muskegon MI 49440	(616) 722-0278 Year-round Mon.–Fri., 9:30–4:30 Weekends, 12:30–4:30	Y	Y	Y	Y

The museum has four permanent galleries—Indian and fur trade, lumbering, "Bodyworks," and natural history—as well as several changing galleries and a sports hall of fame. The county also operates the free C. H. Hackley 2 Hose Co. Fire Barn Museum at 510 W. Clay Ave., a reconstructed, late nineteenth-century firehouse that displays historic fire fighting equipment and photos about Muskegon's disastrous fires.

Muskegon Museum of Art 296 W. Webster Ave. Muskegon MI 49440	(616) 722-2600 Year-round Tues.–Fri., 10–5 Weekends, Noon–5	Y	Y	Y	Y

The permanent collection includes American and French impressionist paintings, Old Masters, contemporary prints, sculpture, glass works, tapestry, and photographs. Durer, Pissarro, Rembrandt, Chase, Bellows, Homer, Degas, Hopper, Curry, Wyeth, Blakelock, and Whistler are among the artists represented. In addition, the galleries display a variety of temporary exhibits.

Owasippe Museum 9900 Russell Road Twin Lake MI 49437	(616) 894-4061 Mid-June–mid-August Daily, 9–4	Y	N	N	N

Founded by the Chicago Area Council of Boy Scouts, the museum features Scouting memorabilia, with uniforms, photos, art on Scouting themes, camping gear, logging implements, and memorabilia.

Osceola County

Evart Public Library and Museum 104 N. Main Box 576 Evart MI 49631	(616) 734-5542 Year-round Mon.–Fri., 9–4:30 Saturday, 9–Noon	N	N	N	Y

Most artifacts are related to local history, including early logging tools that reflect the community's logging heritage. Also in the collection are hundreds of photographs and a mastodon bone recovered in the area.

Wexford County

Johnson Hunting and Fishing Center 6087 E. M-115 Cadillac MI 49601	(616) 779-1321 Memorial Day–Labor Day Tues.–Sun., 10–8 Labor Day–Memorial Day Thurs.–Sun., 10–5	Y	Y	Y	N

There are dioramas and displays of wildlife, including exhibits about the eras of exploitation and conservation, and a tank of native freshwater fish. Slide shows and demonstrations are offered. A foot trail leads from the back door of the center to the Heritage Fisheries and Wildlife Nature Study Area. Although the museum is part of Mitchell State Park, no park permit is necessary to visit.

UPPER PENINSULA

Alger County

Grand Marais Maritime Museum Coast Guard Point Box 395 Grand Marais MI 49839	(906) 494-2669 July 1–Labor Day Daily, 10–5	Y	Y	N	N

The museum is run by the National Park Service as part of Pictured Rocks National Lakeshore on the Lake Superior coast. Its collection includes turn-of-the-century Grand Marais fishing industry artifacts and a Fresnel lens from the Au Sable Light Station. In addition, there are exhibits about shipwrecks, the U.S. Life Saving Service, lighthouses, and the early years of commercial shipping in the region (for more information about Pictured Rocks National Lakeshore, see chap. 1).

Chippewa County

Drummond Island Historical (906) 493-5224 N N N Y
 Museum May 30–Oct. 1
Box 206 Daily, 1–5
Drummond Island MI 49726
Housed in a log building, the collection has furniture, native American artifacts, rocks, and minerals.

Point Iroquois Light Station (906) 437-5272 N Y N Y
Hiawatha National Forest May 15–Oct. 15
Rte. 1, Lakeshore Drive Daily, 10–7
Brimley MI 49783

The Point Iroquois Light Station in Hiawatha National Forest portrays lighthouse history, technology, and the daily life of lightkeepers and their families. As a museum brochure notes,

> Despite hard work and long hours, life at Point Iroquois had its advantages. Compared with more isolated stations, Point Iroquois offered space and a homelike atmosphere. With increased water traffic, it was necessary to expand personnel. By 1908, the light station housed a head keeper, two assistants and their families. They formed their own self-sustaining community complete with a schoolhouse and a teacher for their children.

The light was replaced in 1962 by an automatic signal beacon across Whitefish Bay at Gros Cap, Ontario. Visitors can climb 72 steps to the top of the 65-foot brick tower for a view of Lake Superior, and can walk wildflower-lined paths from the lighthouse to the stony beach. It's on the National Register of Historic Places (for more information about Hiawatha National Forest, see chap. 5).

MUSEUMS

Delta County

Delta County Historical Museum Sand Point Box 484 Escanaba MI 49829	(906) 786-3428 June 1–Labor Day Daily, 1–9	Y	N	N	Y

The museum features displays and exhibits pertinent to local resources, industry, logging, railroads, and the county's relationship to the land and lakes. There is an extensive clothing collection, as well as a 1905 motor launch.

William Bonifas Fine Arts Center 700 First Ave. Escanaba MI 49829	(906) 786-3833 Year-round Mon.–Fri., Noon–4 Sunday, 10–5	Y	Y	N	Y

The Upper Peninsula's only multidisciplinary arts center includes a two-story gallery. Exhibits change monthly and feature regional and national collections. Works from the permanent collection are displayed periodically.

Gogebic County

Old Depot Park Museum Old Depot Park Box 553 Ironwood MI 49938	Memorial Day–Labor Day Daily, Noon–4	N	N	N	Y

The century-old railway passenger depot has been restored for use as a museum depicting local mining and railroad history. Open air band concerts and other events are held here.

Houghton County

Finnish-American Heritage Center (906) 487-7347   Y   Y   N   Y
601 Quincy   Year-round
Hancock MI 49930   Mon.–Fri., 9–4

Located on the campus of Suomi College, the center has an internationally known collection of artifacts, photos, and documents about Finland and Finnish-Americans.

Mackinac County

Iron Industry Museum   (906) 475-7857   Y   Y   Y   N
73 Forge Road   May 1–Oct. 1
Negaunee MI 49866   Daily, 9:30–4:30

The museum, overlooking the Carp River where the Lake Superior region's first iron forge was located, offers exhibits about the region's iron mining and iron miners, ore processing and transportation, and the ethnic background of those who settled in the Upper Peninsula's iron range communities. There's an audiovisual presentation, "Life on the Michigan Iron Ranges," outdoor interpretive trails, and annual special events, including Iron Heritage Day.

Schoolcraft County

Schoolcraft County   (906) 341-5171   Y   Y   N   N
  Historical Society   or 341-2006
Pioneer Park, M-94   May–September
Box 284   Mon.–Fri., 10–4
Manistique MI 49854

Two buildings, a museum house and a log cabin, are filled with antiques, artifacts of logging days and early settlers, furniture, and pictures.

FREE VIEW: MICHIGAN IRON INDUSTRY MUSEUM, NEGAUNEE

Workers once sweated, struggled, dreamed, and anguished as they battled weather and isolation here in the failed hopes of winning wealth from iron. Sounds of wind and birds survive the disappearance of the creaking waterwheel and pounding hammer at the site of the first iron forge in the Lake Superior region.

Now the Michigan Iron Industry Museum lures visitors to a quiet bend of the winding, placid Carp River, a spot that hardly seems to have the makings of a major industrial birthplace.

The water-powered Carp River Forge has been silent since 1855, but the museum traces the human and geological history that led to its construction and abandonment.

It all began 3 billion years ago, when volcanic action created rock containing iron. The next step didn't come until 1844, when government surveyor William Burt's magnetic compass needle jumped. "Look around and see what you can find," Burt ordered his crew. What they found were outcrops of rich iron ore.

Capitalism quickly took over. In 1846, the Jackson Mine opened, followed a year later by the Carp River Forge, which manufactured wrought iron from the ore. Only seven years later the forge closed, a financial flop—"It made little iron and less money," one observer said—and the iron magnates recognized it was more profitable to ship ore elsewhere for processing.

To reach the building from the parking area, I followed a boardwalk lined with aromatic pines, wildflowers, and ferns. The sun and a dim half-moon shared the cloudless noontime sky.

The best way to begin a visit is with the narrated slide show. It reviews the history of Upper Peninsula iron mining and, most interestingly, the ways of life of workers and their families.

Displays and artifacts track the discovery of iron ore, the evolution of mining and shipping the ore, and the economics of a Michigan industry that earned $48 billion in 15 years—contrasted with a mere $955 million for California's gold mines in the same period.

Excerpts from memoirs and letters accompany life-size photos of nineteenth-century people of the region, including miners, a railroad brakeman, a banker, a mule teamster, and a Great Lakes ship captain.

Other exhibits explain the union movement in the mines, the role of company towns, and the activities of women in mining communities.

One display highlights the Upper Peninsula's ethnic mix. The booming mines of the eighteenth and early nineteenth centuries lured immigrants from Cornwall, Sweden, Finland, Ireland, Italy, Canada, Poland, and Germany. By 1910, 90 percent of the workers were foreign born. Only two iron mines still operate in the region, but ethnic diversity remains a lasting legacy of the dreams and nightmares that were mined with the ore.

Outside the museum stands the steam-powered Yankee, the mechanical successor to the mules that originally hauled ore cars at the Jackson Mine. Also outside is a stone memorial to the 51 men who died at the Barnes-Hecker Mine cave-in in nearby Ishpeming more than six decades ago. There was only one survivor.

End your visit with a walk along the short trail overlooking the Carp River. Although the forge has disappeared, with imagination you can still see and smell the charcoal smoke and hear the ringing of the hammer.

Chapter 9

Orchestra, Theater, and Dance Performances

Music, theater, and dance help make the world go round. They're essential elements of our culture and society, whether performed professionally or by talented amateurs. These organizations present free productions at least once each year and often more frequently. In addition, some orchestras have free preconcert presentations by musicians, composers, conductors, and other speakers, as well as theater tours, special children's programs, and ensemble performances. The number of annual free concerts listed is an average because schedules and commitments vary from year to year. Not included are groups that limit their free performances to schools, senior centers, nursing homes, or similar settings.

Many community bands present free concerts across Michigan. They most often can be heard in parks, shopping malls, schools, or festivals. Their schedules usually appear in local newspapers. Newspapers and radio public service spots also announce upcoming free plays, concerts, and recitals by elementary and secondary school students. Colleges with orchestras, choirs, dance companies, and drama groups that put on free performances are listed in chapter 11.

SOUTHEAST

Oakland County

Actors Alliance Theatre Company   (313) 642-1326
30800 Evergreen
Southfield MI 48076

Eight to ten free performances and two to three staged readings a year. Free tours.

Birmingham-Bloomfield (313) 645-2276
   Symphony Orchestra
1592 Buckingham
Birmingham MI 48009

One free concert a year. Free tours.

Oakland Youth Orchestra (313) 858-1985
2100 Pontiac Lake Road
Waterford MI 48328-2735

Three free concerts a year. Free tours.

Scandinavian Symphony (313) 569-0844
c/o Mary Thompson Cultural
   Resource Center
25630 Evergreen Road
Southfield MI 48075

Number of free concerts varies.

Serpent's Tooth Theatre (313) 437-3264
27845 Martindale Road
New Hudson MI 48165-9601

Three free staged readings a year in its New Play Series.

Washtenaw County

Ann Arbor Symphony Orchestra (313) 994-4801
Box 1412
Ann Arbor MI 48106

One free concert a year. Free tours.

People Dancing (313) 930-1949
111 Third St.
Ann Arbor MI 48103

One free performance a year. Spectators are also allowed in the studio to watch works in progress on specific dates. Free tours.

ORCHESTRA, THEATER, AND DANCE PERFORMANCES

Wayne County

Allen Park Symphony Orchestra   (313) 381-1111
Box 145
Allen Park MI 48101

Free Christmas concert.

Livonia Youth Philharmonic   (313) 455-3014 or 453-8887
Box 530601
Livonia MI 48153

Number of free concerts varies.

Mme. Cadillac Dance Theatre   (313) 875-6354
15 E. Kirby Ave.
Detroit MI 48202

Three free performances a year, as well as appearances at special events such as festivals and parades.

SOUTHWEST

Kalamazoo County

Kalamazoo Symphony Orchestra   (616) 349-7759
426 S. Park St.
Kalamazoo MI 49007

Three free summer concerts.

Kent County

Kent Philharmonia Orchestra   (616) 771-3940
143 Bostwick N.E.
Grand Rapids MI 49503

One free concert a year at annual June Arts Festival.

CENTRAL

Bay County

Bay City Players (517) 893-5555
1214 Columbus Ave.
Bay City MI 48706

Five free dress rehearsals a year. Free tours.

Genesee County

Flint Youth Symphony Orchestra (313) 238-9651
1025 E. Kearsley St.
Flint MI 48503

Three free concerts a year.

Flint Symphony Orchestra (313) 238-9651
1025 E. Kearsley St.
Flint MI 48503

Three free summer park concerts a year.

Ingham County

Boarshead: Michigan Public Theater (517) 484-7805 or 484-7800
425 S. Grand Ave.
Lansing MI 48933

Two or three free performances and six to eight free staged readings a year.

Greater Lansing Symphony Orchestra (517) 487-5001
230 N. Washington Square, Suite 315
Lansing MI 48933

Twenty to thirty free ensemble performances a year, plus a Messiah singalong at the Wharton Center for the Performing Arts each December.

Saginaw County

Pit and Balcony Theatre (517) 754-6587
805 N. Hamilton
Saginaw MI 48602

No free performances, but free tours are available.

Saginaw Symphony Orchestra (517) 755-6471
Box 415
Saginaw MI 48606

Two free concerts a year in the Saginaw Civic Center.

Saginaw Symphony Youth Orchestra (517) 755-6641
Box 415
Saginaw MI 48606

Four free concerts a year at Arthur Hill High School.

NORTHEAST

Cheboygan County

Cheboygan Opera House (616) 627-5432
403 N. Huron St.
Box 95
Cheboygan MI 49721

No free performances, but free tours are available.

NORTHWEST

Grand Traverse County

Interlochen Arts Camp (616) 276-6230
Box 199
Interlochen MI 49684

Ten to twenty free concerts each year by five orchestras during the Interlochen Arts Camp and by one orchestra during the Interlochen Arts Academy. Free tours.

Wexford County

Cadillac Area Symphony Orchestra
Box 435
Cadillac MI 49601

Performs at Cadillac Summer Arts Festival.

Interlochen Arts Camp. (Courtesy Interlochen.)

Touring

Chapter 10

Wineries

Michigan ranks fifth in the United States in wine production, and many of its wines have won awards in national and international competitions. A temperate climate moderated by the Great Lakes, coupled with well-drained sandy soil and hilly terrain, make the state an excellent wine-growing region according to the Michigan Grape and Wine Industry Council. Cool winds delay the spring growing season until the risk of early frost has passed, autumn winds prolong the growing season and postpone the frost, and heavy snows bury the vines to insulate them from winter cold. There are four federally recognized viticultural areas in the state especially suitable for wine production: Lake Michigan Shore, Fennville, Leelanau Peninsula, and Old Mission Peninsula.

Popular grape varieties grown on Michigan's 12,500 acres of vineyards include Vignoles, Seyval Blanc, Chardonnay, Chancellor, Foch, de Chaunac, Riesling, Vidal Blanc, Baco Noir, Concord, and Pinot Noir. Vineyards also experiment with other varieties. Some wineries crush only their own grapes, while others also purchase grapes from other Michigan growers.

An ideal time for travelers to enjoy a free tour or tasting is October, when much of the harvest and crushing is under way and fall colors are at their peak.

The following commercial wineries are open to the public for free guided or self-guided tours and for tastings.

SOUTHEAST

Washtenaw County

Sharon Mills Winery (313) 428-9160
5701 Sharon Hollow Road Year-round
Manchester MI 48158 Weekends, Noon–5

Guided tours last 15 minutes at this winery along the River Raisin in Sharon Hollow. The tour covers the stone-walled champagne cellar and 1835 grist mill, which had been restored by Henry Ford for manufacturing cigar lighters and stoplight switches for cars. It was later used as a private home before its conversion to a winery.

SOUTHWEST

Allegan County

Fenn Valley Vineyards
6130 122d Ave.
Fennville MI 49408

(616) 561-2396
Year-round
Mon.–Sat., 10–5
Sunday, 1–5

Guided tours last 30 minutes but are not given during harvest time, September and October. Visitors go into and through the wine cellar.

Harvest time. (Courtesy Michigan Department of Agriculture.)

Self-guided tours can be taken whenever the winery is open. The self-guided tour is from an observation balcony overlooking the wine cellar. Placards explain winemaking equipment and processes, and there is a 17-minute video presentation on harvesting and the proper use and care of wine. Reservations are required for guided tours.

Berrien County

Lemon Creek Winery
533 E. Lemon Creek Road
Berrien Springs MI 49103

(616) 471-1321
April–December
Daily, 9–6

Guided tours last 15 minutes. Visitors tour the vineyard, with a discussion of microclimate and grape varieties, explanation of how wine is made, and demonstration of the bottling line. Reservations are requested for groups.

Madron Lake Hills Winery
14387 Madron Lake Road
Buchanan MI 49107

(616) 695-5660
Year-round
Daily, 11–5

Guided tours last 30 minutes. The winery grows more than 20 commercial and experimental varieties of grapes on three vineyard sites. Reservations are available.

Tabor Hill Winery
185 Mt. Tabor Road
Buchanan MI 49107

(616) 422-1161 or (800) 283-3363
May–September
Mon.–Fri., Noon–4:30
Weekends, 11:30–4:30

Guided tours last 20 minutes. Visitors hear a brief discussion of the winery's history and how the equipment works, then head through the deep cellar to see the bottling line and up into the trophy room where the carvings on the wooden barrels are displayed. Tours can be arranged by appointment after the regular season.

Kalamazoo County

Peterson & Sons Winery
9375 East P Ave.
Kalamazoo MI 49001

(616) 626-9755
Year-round
Mon.–Sat., 10–6
Sunday, Noon–6

Guided tours last 20 minutes, showing how wine is made without the use of sulfites or other chemicals.

Kent County

Le Montueux Vineyard and
  Winery
2365 Eight Mile Road N.W.
Grand Rapids MI 49504

(616) 784-4554
Memorial Day–Dec. 24
Tues.–Sat., 1–6
Hours limited after Labor Day

Guided tours last 20–30 minutes. They cover the complete winemaking process, including, if weather permits, a walk through the vineyard, where French-American hybrid grapes are grown. Reservations are available. Tours outside regular hours are available by appointment.

Van Buren County

St. Julian Wine Co.
716 S. Kalamazoo St.
Box 127
Paw Paw MI 49079

(616) 657-5568
Year-round
Mon.–Sat., 9–5
Sunday, Noon–5

Guided tours last 30 minutes and include the crushing area, production, and vats. There is also a video tour of the vineyard, harvest, and production. In addition, St. Julian, the state's oldest and largest winery, operates free tasting centers in Frankenmuth, Holly, Mackinaw City, Monroe, Parma, Traverse City, Turkeyville, and Union Pier. Reservations are available.

WINERIES

Warner Vineyards
706 S. Kalamazoo St.
Paw Paw MI 49079-0269

(616) 657-3165
Year-round
Mon.–Sat., 9–5
Sunday, Noon–5

Guided tours last 25–30 minutes. Tours at Michigan's second-oldest winery feature a look at the traditional *methode champenoise* style of champagne making. There is a theater presentation on European winemaking. Reservations are requested for groups.

Warner Winery. (Courtesy Michigan Travel Bureau.)

NORTHWEST

Grand Traverse County

Chateau Grand Traverse
12239 Center Road
Traverse City MI 49684

(616) 223-7355 or (800) 283-0247
Year-round
Mon.–Sat., 10–6
Sunday, Noon–6

Guided tours last 30 minutes. They include an overlook of the vineyards, pressing room, cellar, and bottling room, with an explanation of both winemaking and the winery's history.

Leelanau County

Good Harbor Vineyards
M-22
R.1, Box 888
Lake Leelanau MI 49653

(616) 256-7165
May 20–Nov. 1
Mon.–Sat., 11–6
Sunday, Noon–6

There are self-guided tours of the building and equipment at this family-owned winery.

L. Mawby Vineyards
4519 S. Elm Valley Road
Suttons Bay MI 49682

(616) 271-3522
May 1–Oct. 1
Thurs.–Sat., 1–6

Guided tours last 20 minutes to two hours. They cover grape growing, winemaking practices, and the company's "general philosophy of life." Reservations are required.

Leelanau Wine Cellars
12693 Tatch Road
Box 68
Omena MI 49674

(616) 386-5201
Year-round
Mon.–Fri., 10–6
Weekends, 11–5
Winter hours are more limited.

Guided tours last 20 minutes at northern Michigan's largest winery. Visitors see the cellarmaster making wine, barrels, tanks, crush pad, and the bottling room to get an overview of the process. Reservations are available.

FREE VIEW: LEMON CREEK WINERY, BERRIEN SPRINGS

And whence be the grapes of the wine-press which ye tread?
—Lord Thomas Macauley

Vidal, Baco, and Chardonnay grapes hang heavy on the vines here, where the ameliorating climate of nearby Lake Michigan makes it possible for vineyards to thrive. One of six commercial wineries located in the Lake Michigan Shore viticultural region of southwestern Michigan, Lemon Creek offers free tours of its vineyards, winemaking, and bottling process nestled among orchards and ponds.

"Lake Michigan, six miles away, is like a huge solar collector," Cathy Lemon explains as we pass long rows of golden yellow Vidal grapes. The result: winters warm enough to protect the vines, yet with enough snow to insulate them. The Lemon family, including winemaker Jeff and his brother Tim, have farmed here for more than a century.

Cathy Lemon shows off the harvesting equipment and explains how grapes are custom crushed into juice for winemaking. Harvesting generally runs from mid-September through mid-October, depending on weather and the variety of grape ready to be picked.

Come, come; good wine is a good familiar creature, if it be well used.
—William Shakespeare

Currently, 15 to 20 percent of Lemon Creek's annual production from these 95 acres of vines is earmarked for estate-bottled wines. That translates to about 6,000 gallons or 2,000 cases or 24,000 bottles a year. I didn't calculate the number of glasses that much wine would fill. The balance of the crop is sold to other wineries and to do-it-themselves home winemakers. As for the final product, about 85 percent of the dry, semi-dry, semi-sweet, and sweet wines and champagne is sold directly to visitors at the winery, while the rest goes to retailers and restaurants.

Fan the sinking flame of hilarity with the wing of friendship; and pass the rosy wine.
—Charles Dickens

Inside the barn, Lemon walks us through the winemaking process, explaining how bubblers on the stainless steel tanks release the gasses that are created as the juice ferments, turning sugar into alcohol. Visitors learn about racking—moving wine from tank to tank for clarification through the winter—and about how Michigan's cold weather helps stabilize the wine, killing most bacteria naturally. Some of this wine will spend its final month aging in oak barrels.

By May, the previous fall's crop is ready to be bottled, all by hand. For up to two weeks, Lemon family members and winery employees crank up the music in the barn and fill the bottles individually at a rate of 40–45 cases an hour. Lemon's young daughter often runs the hand-corking machine.

Sandalwood, cedarwood, and sweet white wine.
—John Masefield

Barrels and steel tanks where wine is aged. (Courtesy Michigan Department of Agriculture.)

Chapter 11

Colleges and Universities

A wealth of free recreational and cultural opportunities is found on Michigan's public and private college campuses, from tours, plays, and museums to botanical gardens, athletic events, and dance performances. As an example, the Music Department at Michigan State University offers more than 200 free concerts and recitals each year, while its Theatre Department puts on a series of free summer outdoor plays on the banks of the Red Cedar River. From time to time, most campuses have featured speakers, art displays, cultural events, and similar activities.

College newspapers, usually distributed free both on campus and at nearby businesses, are the best source of information about upcoming performances, events, and schedules. If you're on campus, check bulletin boards for event announcements. College public information offices can provide maps, as well as information on such attractions as museums and art galleries.

Campus tours are popular among prospective students, their parents, and alumni, but most schools welcome anybody to come along. Many schools will customize a tour to meet a visitor's particular interests. All those listed in this chapter are open to the general public; excluded are those restricted to potential applicants. Tour policies vary from campus to campus, with some offered at regularly scheduled times and others by appointment. Schedules also may vary due to vacations, semester breaks, or special campus events.

SOUTHEAST

Hillsdale County

Hillsdale College   (517) 437-7341
38 College St.   Private, 1,200 students
Hillsdale MI 49242

Hillsdale College. (Courtesy of Hillsdale College.)

Free Attractions
Campus Tours: Weekdays, (517) 437-7341, extension 355.
Specialized Tours: Sage Center for Fine Arts; Roche Athletic Complex.
Sports Events: Track and field, softball, (517) 437-7364.
Athletic Facilities: Tennis courts.
Concerts, Theater, Dance: (517) 437-7341.
Other: Slayton Arboretum, Center for Constructive Leadership speakers program.

COLLEGES AND UNIVERSITIES   119

Jackson County

Spring Arbor College (517) 750-1200
106 E. Main St. Private, 1,800 students
Spring Arbor MI 49283

Free Attractions
Campus Tours: Monday through Saturday, (800) 748-0011.
Sports Events: Soccer, track and field, tennis, baseball, softball, (517) 750-1200, extension 600.
Athletic Facilities: Tennis courts, track.
Concerts: Band, jazz band, choir, chamber singers, (517) 750-1200, extension 507.

Lenawee County

Siena Heights College (517) 263-0731
1247 E. Siena Heights Drive Private, 1,800 students
Adrian MI 49221

Free Attractions
Campus Tours: Weekdays, 45 minutes, (517) 263-0731, extension 214.
Sports Events: Baseball, softball, tennis, track and field, soccer, volleyball, (517) 263-0731, extension 286.
Theater, Dance: (517) 263-0731, extension 312.
Concerts: Freetime Jazz Ensemble, (517) 263-0731, extension 263; Chamber Ensemble, (517) 263-0731, extension 232.

Monroe County

Monroe County Community (313) 242-7300
   College Public, 3,600 students
1555 S. Raisinville Road
Monroe MI 48161

Free Attractions
Campus Tours: Weekdays, 30 minutes, (313) 242-7300.
Concerts, Theater, Dance: Humanities/Social Sciences Division, (313) 242-7300, extension 345; Community Relations, (313) 242-7300, extension 200.
Museum: Campbell Learning Resources Gallery, (313) 242-7300.

Oakland County

Lawrence Technological (313) 356-0200
  University Private, 5,500 students
21000 W. Ten Mile Road
Southfield MI 48075-1058

Free Attractions
Campus Tours: Weekdays, 30 minutes, (313) 356-0200, extension 3160.
Other: Annual campuswide open house, with hundreds of student displays and demonstrations.

Michigan Christian College (313) 651-5800 or (800) 872-2579
800 W. Avon Road Private, 245 students
Rochester Hills MI 48307

Free Attractions
Campus Tours: Weekdays, 1 hour, (313) 651-5800.
Sports Events: Women's basketball and volleyball, men's basketball, track, baseball, coed soccer, (313) 651-5800.
Concerts: A Capella Choir, (313) 651-5800.

Washtenaw County

Concordia College (313) 995-7300
4090 Geddes Road Private, 500 students
Ann Arbor MI 48105

Free Attractions
Campus Tours: Daily, 1 hour. Tours include Manor House, Chapel of the Holy Trinity with its French stained glass windows, and the Fine Arts Building with its gallery and theater, (313) 995-7317.
Museum: Art gallery, (313) 995-3612.
Concerts: (313) 995-7317.

COLLEGES AND UNIVERSITIES 121

Eastern Michigan University   (313) 487-2227
Ypsilanti MI 48197   Public, 25,000 students

Free Attractions
Campus Tours: Weekdays at 10 A.M. and 2 P.M.; Saturdays at 10 A.M., 1½ hours. Tours include a campus video, presentation from an admissions counselor, and visits to dorms, classrooms, and Recreation/Intramural Building. Academic department tours are available on request. Preregistration preferred, (313) 487-1111.
Specialized Tours: Recreation/Intramural Building, (313) 487-1338.
Sports Events: Gymnastics, tennis, baseball, track, soccer, swimming, golf, volleyball, wrestling, softball, cross-country, diving, (313) 487-2282.
Athletic Facilities: Tennis courts.
Concerts: Orchestra, (313) 487-2448; choir, (313) 487-0280; band, (313) 487-1430.

University of Michigan   (313) 764-1817
Ann Arbor MI 48109   Public, 36,300 students

Free Attractions
Campus Tours: Weekdays, 1 hour. Tours include the central campus, Michigan Union, Burton Memorial Tower, (313) 764-0384.
Specialized Tours: Bentley Historical Library, (313) 764-3482; Clements Library of Americana, (313) 764-2347; Phoenix Memorial Laboratory and Ford Nuclear Reactor, (313) 764-6220.
Athletic Facilities: Tennis courts, track.
Museums: Kelsey Museum of Archaeology, (313) 764-9304; Exhibit Museum, (313) 764-0478; Museum of Art, (313) 764-0395; Stearns Collection of Musical Instruments, (313) 763-4389; Slusser Gallery, (313) 936-2082.
Arboretum: Nichols Arboretum.
Concerts: School of Music, (313) 763-4726.
Theater, Dance: Dance Department, (313) 763-5460; Theatre Department, (313) 764-5350.
Other: Movies, (313) 763-FILM; Ann Arbor Art Fair; Top of the Park.

Washtenaw Community College   (313) 973-3300
4800 E. Huron River Drive   Public, 10,900 students
Box D-1
Ann Arbor MI 48106

Free Attractions
Campus Tours: Weekdays, 1 hour. Weekend tours can be arranged. Tours include student services areas, Learning Resource Center, labs, Auto Center, Business and Industry Center, Campus Events Building, culinary arts, nursing, music classes, (313) 973-3532 or 973-3676.
Specialized Tours: Library, (313) 973-3300.

Wayne County

Henry Ford Community College   (313) 271-2750
5101 Evergreen   Public, 16,000 students
Dearborn MI 48128-1495

Free Attractions
Campus Tours: Weekdays, 1 hour. Tours include library, fine arts center, courtyard, (313) 845-9613.
Sports Events: Basketball, baseball, tennis, volleyball, softball, (313) 845-9647.
Athletic Facilities: Tennis courts, track.
Museums: Sisson Art Gallery, (313) 845-9634.
Concerts, Theater, Dance: Performing Arts Department, (313) 845-9634.
Other: Children's Theatre, (313) 845-9634; Children's Christmas Dance Concert, (313) 845-6314; Women's Recognition Week, (313) 845-9629; Cultural Activities Program films and lectures, (313) 845-9716.

Madonna University   (313) 591-5000
36600 Schoolcraft Road   Private, 4,400 students
Livonia MI 48150

Free Attractions
Athletic Facilities: Tennis courts.
Concerts: (313) 591-5097.
Other: Art exhibits, cultural events.

COLLEGES AND UNIVERSITIES

Marygrove College　　　　　　(313) 862-8000
8425 W. McNichols Road　　　Private, 1,300 students
Detroit MI 48221-2599

Free Attractions
Campus Tours: (313) 862-5200.
Theater, Dance: (313) 862-8000, extension 283.
Concerts: (313) 862-8000, extension 316.
Museum: Art gallery, (313) 862-8000.

Schoolcraft College　　　　　(313) 462-4400
18600 Haggerty Road　　　　Public, 9,500 students
Livonia MI 48152

Free Attractions
Campus Tours: Weekdays, 30 minutes. Tours include physical education facility, Art Department, and award-winning Culinary Arts Department, (313) 462-4463.

University of Detroit Mercy　(313) 993-1000
Box 19900　　　　　　　　　Private, 7,900 students
Detroit MI 48219

Free Attractions
Campus Tours: Weekdays, 40 minutes, (313) 993-1245.
Sports Events: Baseball, softball, soccer, (313) 993-1700.
Athletic Facilities: Tennis courts.

University of Michigan–Dearborn　(313) 593-5000
4901 Evergreen Road　　　　　　Public, 8,000 students
Dearborn MI 48128-1491

Free Attractions
Campus Tours: Weekdays, (313) 593-5100.
Specialized Tours: Spring garden walks, nature walks, and environmental study area, (313) 593-5338.
Sports Events: Women's basketball and volleyball, men's basketball.
Museum: Mardigan Library Baccarat crystal collection, (313) 593-5087.
Concerts: Choir, (313) 593-5138.

University of Detroit Mercy. (Courtesy of University of Detroit Mercy.)

Other: Art exhibitions, (313) 593-5087; films, musicians, comedians, (313) 593-5390.

Wayne State University   (313) 577-2424
Detroit MI 48202   Public, 34,000 students

Free Attractions

Campus Tours: Two days a month, 30–45 minutes. Tours include the main campus, library, Engineering Building, State Hall, Cohn Hall, Campus Hall, (313) 577-3444.

COLLEGES AND UNIVERSITIES

Sports Events: Baseball, softball, tennis, golf, (313) 577-4280 or 577-0182.
Athletic Facilities: Pool, tennis courts, track.
Concerts: (313) 577-1795.
Theater, Dance: (313) 577-5342.
Other: Racquetball and squash courts.

SOUTHWEST

Berrien County

Lake Michigan College (616) 927-3571
2755 E. Napier Ave. Public, 3,600 students
Benton Harbor MI 49022

Free Attractions
Campus Tours: Weekdays, 30 minutes. Tours include library, Mendel Center for Arts and Technology, career and skill enhancement centers, classrooms, (616) 927-3571.
Athletic Facilities: Tennis courts, track.
Museum: Art gallery.
Concerts, Theater, Dance: (616) 927-1221.
Other: Poetry readings; annual Community Arts and Cultural Festival.

Calhoun County

Albion College (517) 629-1000
611 E. Porter St. Private, 1,700 students
Albion MI 49224

Free Attractions
Sports Events: Women's basketball, volleyball, soccer, swimming, tennis, softball, men's soccer, swimming, baseball, tennis, (517) 629-0452.
Athletic Facilities: Track.
Museum: Bobbitt Visual Arts Center.
Concerts: Choir, orchestra, symphonic band, jazz band, (517) 629-0481.
Other: Whitehouse Nature Center, (517) 629-2030.

Cass County

Southwestern Michigan College (616) 782-5113
58900 Cherry Grove Road Public, 2,800 students
Dowagiac MI 49047

Free Attractions
Campus Tours: Weekdays, 45 minutes to 1 hour. Tours include the Fine Arts Building, library, and other buildings on request, (616) 782-5113.
Sports Events: Basketball, softball, cross-country, volleyball, track, wrestling, (616) 782-5113, extension 210.
Museum: (616) 782-5113, extension 334.
Concerts: (616) 782-5113.

Kalamazoo County

Kalamazoo Valley Community (616) 372-5000
  College Public, 9,400 students
6767 West O Ave.
Kalamazoo MI 49009

Free Attractions
Campus Tours: Appointment required, (616) 372-5346.
Sports Events: Women's softball and tennis, men's baseball, tennis, golf, (616) 372-5395.
Athletic Facilities: Pool, tennis courts, track.
Museum: Kalamazoo Public Museum, (616) 345-7092.
Other: Valley Art Show; Black History Month events.

Western Michigan University (616) 387-1000
Kalamazoo MI 49008 Public, 28,000 students

Free Attractions
Campus Tours: 90 minutes. Tours include academic facilities and residence halls, (616) 387-2000.
Sports Events: Baseball, softball, gymnastics, soccer, track, tennis, (616) 387-8620.
Athletic Facilities: Track.
Concerts: (616) 387-5811.
Dance: (616) 387-5811.

COLLEGES AND UNIVERSITIES

Other: Art exhibitions, (616) 387-2436; Michigan Youth Arts Festival, (616) 387-5811.

Kent County

Aquinas College	(616) 459-8281
1607 Robinson Road S.E.	Private, 2,600 students
Grand Rapids MI 49506-1799	

Free Attractions
Sports Events: Basketball, softball, baseball, soccer, track, golf, volleyball, tennis, (616) 459-8281, extension 3101.
Museum: Art gallery, (616) 459-8281.
Botanical Garden: Holmdene Garden, (616) 459-8281.
Concerts: (616) 459-8281.

Calvin College	(616) 957-6000
3201 Burton S.E.	Private, 4,000 students
Grand Rapids MI 49546	

Free Attractions
Campus Tours: Weekdays, 1 hour, (616) 957-6106.
Specialized Tours: Art gallery, (616) 957-6326; observatory, (616) 957-6435; nature preserve, (616) 957-6497.
Sports Events: Soccer, cross-country, golf, swimming, tennis, track, baseball, volleyball, hockey, field hockey, (616) 957-6176.
Athletic Facilities: Tennis courts, track.
Museum: Art gallery, (616) 957-6326; Heritage Hall, (616) 957-6313; Meeter Center for Calvin Studies, (616) 957-7081.
Nature Preserve: (616) 957-6497.
Concerts: Music Department, (616) 957-6253 or 957-6411.
Theater: Improv Team, (616) 957-6283.
Dance: Dance Guild, (616) 957-6176.

Grand Rapids Community College   (616) 771-4000
143 Bostwick N.E.   Public, 13,000 students
Grand Rapids MI 49503

Free Attractions
Campus Tours: Weekdays, 1 hour. Tours include the Applied Technology Center, Hospitality Education, and Ford Fieldhouse, (616) 771-4000.
Athletic Facilities: Swimming pool, tennis courts, track.

Kendall College of Art and Design   (616) 451-2787
111 Division Ave.   Private, 650 students
Grand Rapids MI 49503-3194

Free Attractions
Campus Tours: Weekdays, 45 minutes. Tours include the gallery, working classes, and hall displays of student art, (616) 451-2787.
Museum: Gallery, (616) 451-2787.

Ottawa County

Grand Valley State University   (616) 895-6611
Campus Drive   Public, 13,000 students
Allendale MI 49401

Free Attractions
Campus Tours: Weekdays year-round and Saturdays from October to April, 1 hour, (800) 748-0246 or (616) 895-2025.
Specialized Tours: Cook-DeWitt Center, (616) 895-3596; Zumberge Library, (616) 895-3252; Fieldhouse, (616) 895-3259.
Sports Events: Baseball, softball, tennis, (616) 895-3800.
Athletic Facilities: Tennis courts, track.
Concerts, Theater, Dance: Arts Hotline, (616) 895-3610 or 895-3668; Music Department, (616) 895-3484.
Other: Lectures, exhibits.

COLLEGES AND UNIVERSITIES

Hope College (616) 392-5111
Holland MI 49423 Private, 2,700 students

Free Attractions
Campus Tours: Weekdays, 30 minutes. Historical tours highlight the growth of the campus, (616) 394-7860.
Specialized Tours: Dimnent Memorial Chapel, (616) 394-7860.
Sports Events: Track, golf, soccer, volleyball, baseball, tennis, swimming, softball, (616) 394-7690.
Museum: Joint Archives of Holland, (616) 394-7798.
Concerts: Music Department, (616) 394-7650.
Other: DePree Art Center gallery exhibitions.

St. Joseph County

Glen Oaks Community College (616) 467-9945
62249 Shimmel Road Public, 1,400 students
Centreville MI 49032

Free Attractions
Campus Tours: Weekdays, 1–1½ hours, (616) 467-9945.
Athletic Facilities: Tennis courts.

CENTRAL

Bay County

Delta College (517) 686-9000
University Center MI 48710 Public, 11,200 students

Free Attractions
Campus Tours: Weekdays, (517) 686-9092.
Sports Events: Basketball, volleyball, soccer, softball, (517) 686-9477.
Athletic Facilities: Tennis courts, track.
Museum: Fine Arts Galleria, (517) 686-9000.
Concerts: (517) 686-9087.
Other: Planetarium, (517) 686-9412.

Genesee County

GMI Engineering and Management Institute (313) 762-9500
1700 W. Third Ave.   Private, 3,100 students
Flint MI 48504

Free Attractions
Campus Tours: Weekdays, 1½ hours, (313) 762-7865.
Specialized Tours: Humanities Art Gallery, (313) 762-7976.
Museum: Alumni Foundation Historical Collection, (313) 762-9890.
Other: PACE series of visiting cultural and educational programs with speakers, plays, dance, and concerts.

Mott Community College   (313) 762-0200
1401 E. Court St.   Public, 10,900 students
Flint MI 48503

Free Attractions
Campus Tours: 30 minutes, (313) 762-0940.
Specialized Tours: Library, athletic facilities, gardens.
Athletic Facilities: Tennis courts, fitness trail.
Museum: Chester H. Wilson Geology Museum, (313) 762-0500.
Concerts: (313) 762-0459.
Other: Guest lecturers and performers, (313) 762-0497.

University of Michigan–Flint   (313) 762-3000
303 E. Kearsley St.   Public, 6,600 students
Flint MI 48502

Free Attractions
Campus Tours: Weekdays, 1 hour. Tours include classroom and lab facilities, Recreation Building, and Student Center, (313) 762-3431.
Specialized Tours: Library, (313) 762-3400; Recreation Building, (313) 762-3441.
Concerts: (313) 762-3377.
Other: Comedy series, music series, art gallery exhibits, public forums.

COLLEGES AND UNIVERSITIES

Gratiot County

Alma College (517) 463-7111
Alma MI 48801-1599 Private, 1,200 students

Free Attractions
Campus Tours: Weekdays, 1 hour. Tours include the chapel, academic buildings, library, Science Center, and athletic complex, (517) 463-7139.
Athletic Facilities: Tennis courts.
Museum: Flora Kirsch Beck Art Gallery, (517) 463-7220.
Concerts: Music Department, (517) 463-7167.

Ingham County

Michigan State University (517) 355-1855
East Lansing MI 48824 Public, 43,300 students

Free Attractions
Campus Tours: Monday through Saturday, 1 hour. By foot and bus, tours include the central campus, residence halls, classrooms, athletic facilities, university farms, and other requested sites, (517) 355-4458.
Specialized Tours: Wharton Center for Performing Arts, most Sundays except during the summer, (517) 336-2000; Abrams Planetarium, (517) 355-4632; MSU Museum, (517) 355-2370; Kresge Art Museum, (517) 355-7631; Jack Breslin Student Events Center, (517) 336-2000; MSU Kellogg Biological Station, (616) 671-2412.
Sports Events: Tennis, golf, track and field, cross country, fencing, (517) 355-2271.
Athletic Facilities: Track.
Museums: MSU Museum, (517) 355-2730; Kresge Art Museum, (517) 355-7631.
Botanical Gardens: W. J. Beal Botanical Garden, Horticultural Garden, All-American Trial Garden.
Theater: (517) 355-0148.
Concerts: (517) 355-3345.
Other: Abrams Planetarium exhibit hall, (517) 355-4632.

Isabella County

Central Michigan University   (517) 774-4000
Mt. Pleasant MI 48859   Public, 18,000 students

Free Attractions
Campus Tours: Monday–Saturday, 1 hour, (517) 774-3076.
Museum: Center for Cultural and Natural History, (517) 774-3829.
Concerts: Music Department, (517) 774-3281.
Other: Clarke Historical Library, (517) 774-3352.

Mecosta County

Ferris State University   (616) 592-2000
901 S. State St.   Public, 12,400 students
Big Rapids MI 49307

Free Attractions
Campus Tours: Weekdays at 1 P.M., 1–1½ hours, (616) 592-3963.
Sports Events: Softball, bulldog baseball, tennis, swimming, (616) 592-2860.
Athletic Facilities: Pool, track, tennis courts.
Museum: Rankin Center University Art Gallery, (616) 592-2000.
Concerts: Music Center, (616) 592-2501.
Other: Astronomical viewings in Rawlinson Observatory, winter Festival of Arts.

Montcalm County

Montcalm Community College   (517) 328-2111
2800 College Drive S.W.   Public, 2,000 students
Box 300
Sidney MI 48885-0300

Free Attractions
Campus Tours: Weekdays, (517) 328-2111, extension 224.
Athletic Facilities: Tennis courts.
Concerts: (517) 328-2111, extension 218.
Other: Annual August Heritage Village celebration.

COLLEGES AND UNIVERSITIES

Saginaw County

Saginaw Valley State University (517) 790-4000
University Center MI 48710 Public, 6,200 students

Free Attractions
Campus Tours: Monday–Saturday, 45 minutes. Tours include Marshall Fredericks Sculpture Gallery, Ryder Center for Health and Physical Education, and labs, (517) 790-4200.
Specialized Tours: Marshall Fredericks Sculpture Gallery, (517) 790-5667.
Sports Events: Baseball, softball, track, volleyball, (517) 790-4053.
Athletic Facilities: Tennis courts.
Museum: University Art Gallery, (517) 790-4159.
Concerts: Department of Music, (517) 790-4159.
Theater: Department of Communication and Theatre, (517) 790-4019.

NORTHEAST

Alpena County

Alpena Community College (517) 356-9021
666 Johnson St. Public, 2,400 students
Alpena MI 49707-1495

Free Attractions
Campus Tours: Weekdays, 1 hour, (517) 356-9021, extension 200.

Roscommon County

Kirtland Community College (517) 275-5121
10775 N. St. Helen Road Public, 1,200 students
Roscommon MI 48653

Free Attractions
Campus Tours: Weekdays, 1 hour, (517) 275-5121.

NORTHWEST

Clare County

Mid Michigan Community College   (517) 386-7792
1375 S. Clare Ave.   Public, 2,200 students
Harrison MI 48625

Free Attractions
Campus Tours: Weekdays, 45 minutes, (517) 386-7792, extension 290.
Athletic Facilities: Tennis courts.

Emmet County

North Central Michigan College   (616) 348-6600
1515 Howard St.   Public, 2,000 students
Petoskey MI 49770

Free Attractions
Campus Tours: Weekdays, 30 minutes. Tours include classroom buildings, library, conference center, and dormitories, (616) 348-6605.

Grand Traverse County

Northwestern Michigan College   (616) 922-0650
1701 E. Front St.   Public, 4,400 students
Traverse City MI 49684

Free Attractions
Campus Tours: Weekdays, 1 hour, (616) 922-1400.
Specialized Tours: Library, (616) 922-1061; Rogers Observatory, (616) 922-1113.
Concerts, Theater, Dance: Humanities Division, (616) 922-1332.
Athletic Facilities: Tennis courts.

COLLEGES AND UNIVERSITIES 135

Muskegon County

Muskegon Community College   (616) 773-9131
221 S. Quarterline Road   Public, 5,200 students
Muskegon MI 49442

Free Attractions
Campus Tours: Weekdays, 30 minutes. Tours include the Art and Industrial Technology buildings, various departments, and student areas, including food service areas, (616) 777-0366.
Specialized Tours: Library, (616) 777-0269.
Sports Events: Women's basketball, men's basketball and wrestling, (616) 777-0381.
Concerts: (616) 777-0324.
Museum: Art gallery, (616) 777-0324.
Other: "Nooner" comedy performances, art shows at gallery.

UPPER PENINSULA

Chippewa County

Lake Superior State University   (906) 632-6841
Sault Ste. Marie MI 49783   Public, 3,500 students

Free Attractions
Campus Tours: Monday–Saturday, 1½ hours, (906) 635-2231.
Athletic Facilities: Tennis courts, track.
Concerts: (906) 635-2265.
Other: Ben Long Planetarium shows, (906) 635-2441.

Delta County

Bay de Noc Community College   (906) 786-5802
2001 N. Lincoln Road   Public, 2,300 students
Escanaba MI 49829

Free Attractions
Campus Tours: Weekdays, 1/2–2 hours. Tours include Learning Resources Center, technical training labs, and academic program areas, (906) 786-5802.

Houghton County

Michigan Technological University (906) 487-1885
1400 Townsend Drive   Public, 6,600 students
Houghton MI 49931-1295

Free Attractions
Campus Tours: Weekdays. The 10 A.M. tour of major campus facilities lasts 2½ hours and includes lunch; the 2 P.M. tour lasts 1½ hours, (906) 487-2335.

Northern Michigan University. (Courtesy of Northern Michigan University.)

COLLEGES AND UNIVERSITIES 137

Museum: A. E. Seaman Mineral Museum, (906) 487-2572.
Other: Annual Winter Carnival.

Marquette County

Northern Michigan University   (906) 227-1000
Marquette MI 49855   Public, 8,000 students

Free Attractions
Campus Tours: Mondays, Wednesdays, and Fridays, 40 minutes, (906) 227-1709.
Specialized Tours: Superior Dome, (906) 227-2850; Library, (906) 227-2294; Theater, (906) 227-2553.
Sports Events: Volleyball, swimming, (906) 227-2105.
Athletic Facilities: Track.
Museum: Lee Hall Gallery, (906) 227-1481.

Chapter 12

Industry and Business

From factories to power plants, from mills to craft studios, a variety of Michigan businesses open their doors to tourists, even if you're not planning to buy anything on the spot.

You can expect to be treated courteously, and staffers are generally happy to answer questions or explain their manufacturing process and company history in more detail. However, remember that these are operating businesses, so visitors on tour are not the only priority. Not listed are the many fudge shops, primarily in northern Michigan, where you can watch high-calorie treats being made on marble slabs.

The hours indicated are for tours or demonstrations, but the establishment may be open longer hours or additional days for regular business, including sales to visitors in their shops or factory outlets. Groups are advised to check for reservations.

SOUTHEAST

Monroe County

Detroit Edison Fermi 2 Power Plant (313) 586-5228
6400 N. Dixie Highway Year-round
Newport MI 48166 Mon.–Fri., 8–5
  Saturday, by appointment

Guided tours of this nuclear power plant last 2 to 3 hours and include the control room simulator used for training and drills, as well as the twin 400-foot cooling tours. The visitor center has a scale model of the reactor and its containment structure. Reservations are required.

Oakland County

Davisburg Candle Factory (313) 634-4214
634 Broadway Year-round
Box 8 Mon.–Fri., 10–4:30
Davisburg MI 48350

Demonstrations lasting 20–30 minutes show the taper line for making candles and the color dip tanks for blending colors. The factory specializes in custom colors and long-burning blends of pure wax. Reservations are required.

Washtenaw County

Chelsea Milling Co. (313) 475-1361
201 North St. Year-round
Box 460 Mon.–Fri., 9:30–1:30
Chelsea MI 48118-0460

This is the home of Jiffy mixes. Tours last up to 1½ hours and include a slide presentation, escorted walk through the packaging department and warehouse, and a refreshment period. Reservations are required.

Wayne County

Detroit & Mackinac Brewery Ltd. (313) 831-2739
470 W. Canfield Ave. Year-round
Detroit MI 48201 Mon.–Fri., by appointment

Detroit's only brewery is typical of the national growth of minibreweries that proudly experiment with and produce their own ales and beers for small-scale commercial sale, generally to select restaurants and stores. There are 30-minute guided tours and free samples. Reservations are required.

Mazda Motor Manufacturing
1 Mazda Drive
Flat Rock MI 48134

(313) 782-7800
Year-round
Thursday, 9 and 1:30

A two-hour tour provides an introduction to and guided walks through the auto manufacturing plant and a question-and-answer session. Reservations are required, with 1–2 months' advance written notice requested.

SOUTHWEST

Berrien County

Indiana Michigan Power Co.
Cook Energy Information Center
Red Arrow Highway
Box 115
Bridgman MI 49106

(616) 456-6101
Jan. 15–Dec. 15
Tues.–Sun., 10–5

There are 45-minute guided tours of the center that explain the workings of the nearby 2.1 million-kilowatt Cook Nuclear Power Plant run by

Detroit & Mackinac Brewery Ltd. (Courtesy Detroit & Mackinac Brewery.)

Indiana Michigan Power Co. Included are theater presentations about nuclear energy and power plant operations. On many weekends, the center hosts special exhibits of works and presentations by regional sculptors, wood carvers, quilters, hobbyists, and artists.

Ottawa County

DeKlomp Wooden Shoe and Delftware Factory and Valdheer Tulip Gardens	(616) 399-1900 Year-round
12755 Quincy St.	Mon.–Fri., 8–6
Holland MI 49424	Weekends, 9–5

Twenty-minute guided tours are available. Visitors can see Dutch-style wooden shoes carved here and can watch Delftware molded, fired, handpainted, and glazed and can talk with the artists at the only Delft factory in the United States. During the spring only, there's an admission charge for the tulip farm's show garden.

CENTRAL

Saginaw County

Bronner's Christmas Wonderland	(517) 652-9931
25 Christmas Lane	Year-round
Frankenmuth MI 48734	June 1–Dec. 24,
	Mon.–Fri., 9–9
	Saturday, 9–7
	Sunday, Noon–7
	Dec. 26–May 31
	Mon.–Thurs. and Sat., 9–5:30
	Friday, 9–9
	Sunday, 1–5:30

What can you say about a store that's proven to be a tourism megahit? The packed parking lot and rows of tour buses say it all. Bronner's bills itself as the "world's largest Christmas store," so should its 2 million visitors a year doubt it? The Alpine-design store and 1.5-acre grounds sport Christmas decorations regardless of the calendar, and a mind-boggling array of garlands, lights, and ornaments. Inside are dancing Santas, singing carolers, more than 800 animated figures, and background holiday music. More than 260 Christmas trees are decorated in toyland, religious, and traditional themes, and an 18-minute 10-projector multi-image show is presented throughout the day. Santa, of course, is on duty in December, and the Easter Bunny appears in the spring.

Frankenmuth Flour Mill and General Store   (517) 652-8422
701 Mill St.   Year-round
Frankenmuth MI 48734   Daily, 10–6

There are self-guided, 15-minute tours of this restored flour mill, which was built in 1847 and restored a number of times since then. The mill includes $3^1/_2$ stories of elevators, chutes, automatic scale, sifters, and grinders, with roller mills and grindstone. The equipment is all in working order, and corn is occasionally ground here. A waterwheel, 13 feet in

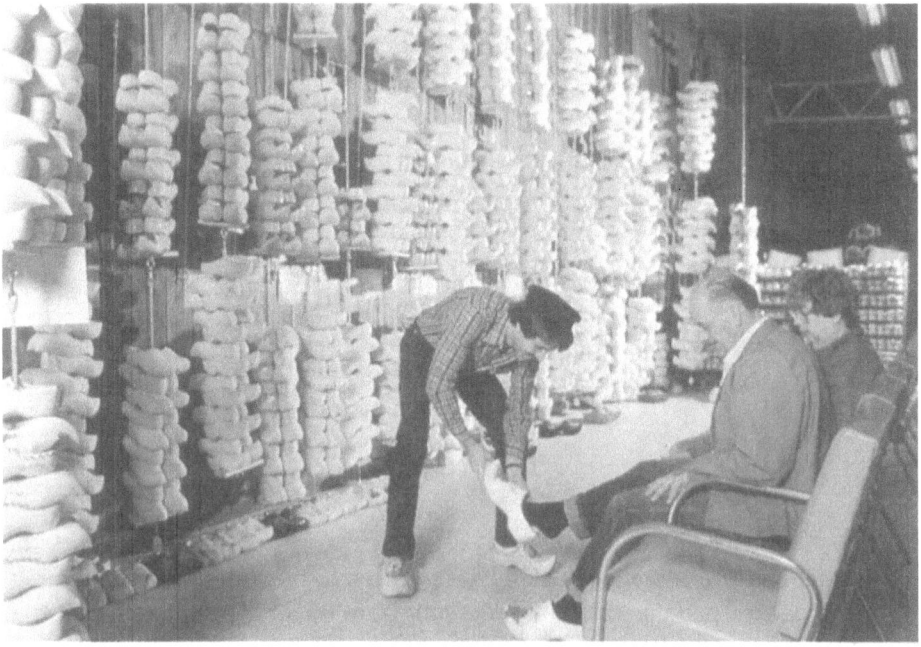

DeKlomp Wooden Shoe and Delftware Factory. (Courtesy DeKlomp Wooden Shoe and Delftware Factory.)

INDUSTRY AND BUSINESS

Bronner's Christmas Wonderland. (Courtesy of Bronner's.)

diameter, develops three horsepower at 13 revolutions per minute. The original mill dam can also be seen.

Frankenmuth Woolen Mill (517) 652-8121
570 S. Main St. Summer
Frankenmuth MI 48734 Daily, 9–9
Winter
Daily, 10–6

A half-hour tour covers the company's century-old history and shows the washing, carding, and spinning of wool, as well as the making of hand-tied wool-filled comforters. Visitors have a chance to hand-spin wool into yarn. The mill also processes mohair, llama, angora, and other exotic fibers. Reservations are required.

Zeilinger Wool Co.
1130 Weiss St.
Frankenmuth MI 48734

(517) 652-2920
Year-round
Mon.–Sat., 9–5:30

Tours last 15–30 minutes. They cover the processing, manufacturing, and laundering of wool and the reprocessing of wool products, the custom making of curtains and decorator pillows, and the hand stitching of pieced quilts. Wool is processed on vintage textile carding machines, each about 75 years old. Visitors can also watch employees make hand-stitched quilts and pillows and hand-tied comforters and woolen mattress pads. Reservations are preferred.

NORTHWEST

Benzie County

Gwen Frostic Prints
5140 River Road
Benzonia MI 49616

(616) 882-5505
May–early November
Daily, 9–5:30
Mid-November–April
Mon.–Sat., 9–4:30

Original block prints on nature themes are made here. The showroom is situated so visitors can see the entire operation. The printing presses used to produce books, postcards, notepaper, napkins, and placemats designed by artist Gwen Frostic are in operation only from 9–4:30 weekdays. Wild bird carvings by many artists are on display, and there is a large nature library.

INDUSTRY AND BUSINESS   **145**

Grand Traverse County

Candle Factory
Grandview Parkway and
　Hall Street
Box 807
Traverse City MI 49685

(616) 946-2280
Year-round
Mon.–Sat., 10–6
Sunday, Noon–5

Visitors can see candles being made in this former turn-of-the-century coal gasification plant facing Grand Traverse Bay. In addition to the year-round hours, the factory is open every evening in July and August, and some evenings from September through December.

Zeilinger Wool Co. (Courtesy Zeilinger Wool Co.)

Newaygo County

Gerber Products Co. (616) 928-2000
445 State St. Year-round
Fremont MI 49413 Mon.–Fri., 9–4

Babies have been the business in Fremont since 1928. Although no factory tours are offered, there is a visitor center that features a three-dimensional movie about Gerber Products, historical pictures, a museum featuring the company and its products, and children's activities and memorabilia. There's even a video that follows the progress of peas from planting to a baby's dish.

Oceana County

Shelby Gem Factory (616) 861-2165
1330 Industrial Drive Year-round
Box 155 Mon.–Fri., 9–5:30
Shelby MI 49455-0155 Saturday, Noon–4

This factory manufactures gems, including simulated diamonds, rubies, emeralds, and sapphires. Its 50-seat theater presents a show about natural and manufactured gems. There are exhibits and displays, and visitors can try their hand at a cutting, or faceting, machine.

UPPER PENINSULA

Delta County

Hoegh Pet Casket Co. (906) 428-2151
317 Delta Ave. Year-round
Box 311 Mon.–Fri., 8–Noon
Gladstone MI 49837 and 1–4

The company manufactures pet caskets, memorial plaques, and monuments. There are 20-minute guided tours through the factory, model pet cemetery, and display room, as well as audiovisual programs.

Chapter 13

Government Attractions

In one sense, government attractions aren't free because, as a taxpayer, you're already paying for them. The good news is that there's no extra charge for these tours.

SOUTHEAST

St. Clair County

U.S. Coast Guard Cutter *Bramble*   (313) 982-2684
Foot of Lincoln Avenue
Box 610786
Port Huron MI 48060

The *Bramble,* still on active duty, is a 180-foot Coast Guard cutter. Since its launching in 1943, it's been based at various times in California, the Aleutian islands, Hawaii, Miami, Detroit, and Puerto Rico. In 1957, the *Bramble* became one of the first ships to circumnavigate North America, and later it was assigned to drug interception duties in the Caribbean. Its current assignment includes maintenance of buoys and lighthouses and service as an icebreaker.

Weekend afternoon tours of the *Bramble* begin at Pine Grove Park and last from 15 minutes to an hour, depending on the number of visitors and how much they want to see and learn. Visitors see the topside and work areas, engine room, buoy deck, galley, and bridge. Hours are subject to change due to operational commitments and emergencies.

Wayne County

Detroit Mounted Police   (313) 876-0061
100 E. Bethune
Detroit MI 48202

The Detroit Police Department offers 30-minute tours at 11 A.M. on weekdays. Visitors are shown police horses, a century-old barn, blacksmith shop, and leather shop, and learn about mounted police operations. Reservations are required.

Detroit Wastewater Treatment　　(313) 297-9187
　Plant
9300 W. Jefferson
Detroit MI 48209

This is the world's largest single-site wastewater treatment plant, serving more than 3 million people in Detroit and dozens of southeastern Michigan communities. An average of 700 million gallons of water are treated here each day.

Guided tours last $1^{1}/_{2}$–2 hours, generally Mondays and Fridays between 8 A.M. and noon and Saturdays between 9 A.M. and 2 P.M. Evening tours also can be scheduled. Participants must be at least 10 years old. The tours cover the primary treatment process and main pump station. Visitors are shown how water is cleaned and disinfected. Special programs are held during Water Quality Awareness Week and Drinking Water Week. Reservations are required.

U.S. District Court　　(313) 226-7200
231 W. Lafayette
Detroit MI 48226

Get a behind-the-scenes look at one of the country's largest federal courthouses. The tour includes the nineteenth-century Chief Judge's Courtroom, with walls and furniture made entirely of Italian marble. Two-hour guided tours are offered weekdays from 8:30 A.M. to 5 P.M. Reservations are required.

CENTRAL

Ingham County

State Capitol　　(517) 373-2353
Tour Guide Service
Lansing MI 48909-7536

The cornerstone of the state's third Capitol was laid in 1873 and the domed building was dedicated on New Year's Day, 1879. The exterior of the building has changed little since then, and much of the interior is restored to its ninteenth-century flavor.

Visitors receive a 45-minute guided tour of public areas, including the Senate and House chambers. Guides highlight the building's history and restoration, as well as the legislative process. Videos about the restoration and legislation are regularly shown. Tours are offered weekdays from 9 A.M. to 5 P.M., Saturdays from 10 A.M. to 5 P.M., and Sundays from noon to 4 P.M. A weekly schedule of concerts, rallies, protests, and demonstrations is available.

NORTHEAST

Cheboygan County

U.S. Coast Guard Cutter *Mackinaw* (616) 627-3181
632 Coast Guard Drive
Cheboygan MI 49721

The cutter *Mackinaw* is open daily for 10-minute tours of the weather-deck and pilot house, from spring through fall, depending on operational needs. Tours are held weekdays from 6 to 8 P.M. and weekends from 9 to 11 A.M. and 1 to 4 P.M.

FREE VIEW: STATE CAPITOL, LANSING

History, civics, architecture, and humor envelop the group as it climbs the grand staircase from the glass-floored Rotunda to the wood-paneled room that housed the Michigan Supreme Court for almost 90 years.

"As we're going up the stairs, a lot of big shots are going down them," our tour guide jokes to a combination of high school students, teachers, and tourists. A passing legislator stops to say hello.

After the Supreme Court moved to a nearby building, its ornate former quarters on the third floor were turned over to the Senate Appropriations Committee. It is, the guide explains, the most powerful and important room in the Capitol because "this is where the bucks are handed out."

To make the point, he recruits a student to portray a witness, then stages an abbreviated simulation of a legislative committee hearing on a

Michigan State Capitol. (Courtesy Michigan Travel Bureau.)

college funding proposal. "Democracy is like playing a great big game of dodge ball. The more people who play, the more fun it is," he tells the group. "You guys are the bosses, you pay the bills."

This hasn't always been the place to come to find money or democracy.

Lansing was a little-explored wilderness in 1847 when the Legislature chose it as a compromise to replace Detroit as the capital city of the young state. And the Capitol that houses Michigan's government today is far different than the territorial courthouse that served as the original seat of government in Detroit, and from the wooden building erected in Lansing in the winter of 1847.

Gazing up from the glass-floored Rotunda toward the elaborate, painted Capitol dome, it's evident how much architect Elijah E. Myers was influenced by the U.S. Capitol in Washington when he designed this building in 1872. The $1.4 million project built of granite, limestone, marble, and sandstone was completed in 1879 and became a model for other states.

Recently restored to its nineteenth-century appearance, the Capitol exudes a sense of formality, tradition, and power.

Glass cases around the first floor of the Rotunda hold battle flags—some scarred and torn from fighting—from Michigan units that served in the Civil War, Spanish-American War, and World War I. Portraits of governors line the Rotunda's second and third floors. Brass doorknobs are emblazoned with the Michigan coat of arms, apple blossoms, or farm scenes, while door hinges boast the coat of arms.

From the vantage point of the balcony-level gallery above the House chamber, visitors look down upon legislators reading or listening at their walnut desks, chatting with aides and colleagues, or standing at their microphones to debate. Looking up from their seats, visitors and representatives alike can see glass panels in the ceiling etched with the seal of each state and the United States. There also are glass panels depicting Johnny Appleseed and an eighth grader's rendition of the Mackinac Bridge.

There are modern touches, however. Computerized voting systems and "scoreboards" have been installed in the House and Senate chambers. Custom-designed chandeliers, originally gas-lit, are now electrified.

Free tours are given almost every day, year-round. Itineraries vary depending on the make-up and interest of each group, and what activities are going on.

Whether or not on an escorted tour, visitors are welcome to sit in the galleries for legislative sessions and to attend committee meetings and hearings in the building. If your timing is right, you also can hear a free school band, choir, or orchestra concert inside or outside the building, and there may be a demonstration with speakers on the east steps.

Outside, landmarks on the Capitol grounds include a white pine, which is the official state tree, as well as monuments to veterans and Michigan participants in the Civil and Spanish-American Wars. In front of the east portico stands a statue of Austin Blair, governor during the Civil War. Near Blair, protected by a black metal fence, is the nation's largest known catalpa, a tree almost as old as the Capitol.

Chapter 14

Walking Tours

One of the best ways to savor the flavor of a community is through a self-guided walking tour. Proceed at your own pace. Take as much time as you want. Look at buildings and parks. Watch people. Take photos. Rest. Enjoy an ice cream cone.

These listings include some, but not all, highlights along each route. Often, buildings along these routes have been restored or converted for other uses, including government and private offices, stores, museums, or apartments. Architectural styles are indicated in parentheses.

In general, these walking tours concentrate on broad local history, with some natural attractions and features also emphasized along the route. A few, however, are more thematically focused: historic churches of Sault Ste. Marie, George Armstrong Custer's ties to Monroe, and sculpture in St. Joseph.

Many privately owned buildings are residences or offices, but some let visitors look through unescorted or on a guided tour. In some communities, such as Manistee, certain buildings along the route are open on a regular schedule; other places may host annual open house days.

This chapter covers more than two-dozen walking tours in a variety of cities and villages, providing a cross-section of how much can be seen on your own in a short time over a short distance. To learn about walking tours elsewhere, contact the local visitor and convention center, chamber of commerce, municipal historic district commission, or historical society.

SOUTHEAST

Monroe County

Monroe's Traces of Gen. George A. Custer. Highlights include the First Methodist Episcopal Church, site of a memorial service for six Monroe soldiers who died at Little Big Horn; Judge Bacon House, where Custer's wife was raised and where the couple lived in 1868; Emanuel Custer House, purchased by his father in 1863; Monroe County Historical Museum, with its collection of Custer memorabilia; and the site of 1853 Tebbins Academy, where he attended school.

There's also a separate historic Monroe walking tour. For a brochure, contact the Monroe County Historical Society, 126 S. Monroe St., Monroe MI 48161, (313) 243-7137.

St. Clair County

Port Huron River Walks. There are three routes along the St. Clair River: Thomas Edison River Walk, beginning under the Blue Water Bridge; Municipal River Walk to the Black River; and Marina Walk. Highlights include ships and boats, marinas, fishing, and river vistas. For a brochure, contact the Port Huron Recreation Department, 2829 Armour St., Port Huron MI 48060, (313) 984-9760.

Washtenaw County

Chelsea Home-Town Heritage. Highlights include the clock tower of the old Glazier Stove Works Building, home of the "Best and Brightest" stove; 1880 Michigan Central Depot (Victorian); 1880 brick Sylvan Township Hall; 1892 Edward Vogel House; and the 1860 Chelsea Library. For a brochure, contact the Chelsea Area Chamber of Commerce, Box 94, Chelsea MI 48118, (313) 475-1145.

Saline. There are two designated walking routes. Highlights include the 1845 Schuyler-Ford-Weller Mill (Greek Revival), 1889 United Methodist Church, 1863 Annin-Peoples House (Italianate), 1887 Wallace Block, 1900 Cool-Compton House (Colonial Revival), 1876 Davenport-Curtiss House (Second Empire), and an 1870 railroad station. For a brochure, contact the Saline Historical District Commission, 100 N. Harris, Box 155, Saline MI 48176, (313) 429-4907.

SOUTHWEST

Berrien County

St. Joseph SculpTur. It leads to nine pieces of sculpture, including the stainless steel Nimbus Flight at the Krasl Art Center, Josephine the bear and her two cubs at the corner of State and Market Streets, a bronze bust of nineteenth-century poet Ben King in Lake Bluff Park, and a bronze father and his two children, titled Sand Castles—What Dreams Are Made Of—in the Margaret Beckley Upton Auditorium. For a brochure, contact the Krasl Art Center, 707 Lake Blvd., St. Joseph MI 49085, (616) 983-0271.

Calhoun County

Battle Creek. There are three historic district tours: Advent Town, Downtown, and Maple Street. Highlights include the 1899–1900 Adventist Hospital, 1886 Kimball House Museum (Queen Anne), sites of abolitionist Sojourner Truth's home and first log cabin school, 1890 Maple United Methodist Church, 1901 Battle Creek Gas Co. (Romanesque), 1911 City Hall, W. K. Kellogg House, 1887–88 Michigan Central depot (Romanesque), 1905 Willard Library (Neoclassical), and a memorial to rock musician Del Shannon. For brochures, contact the Battle Creek Historic District Commission, City Hall, Box 1717, Battle Creek MI 49016, (616) 966-3320.

Marshall. Highlights include the 1860 Honolulu House (Italianate), built by a judge who served as U.S. consul to the Sandwich (now Hawaiian) Islands; 1835 National House Inn (Greek Revival), the oldest operating inn in Michigan; 1914 public library (Vernacular); 1839 James Wright Gordon Governor's Mansion (Greek Revival), built by an interim governor in the vain hope that Marshall would become the state capital; and the 1902 Grand Army of the Republic Hall, now a historic archive. For a brochure, contact the Marshall Historical Society, Box 68, Marshall MI 49068, (616) 781-8544.

Kalamazoo County

Kalamazoo Historic District. Highlights include the 1895 State Hospital Water Tower (Queen Anne); 1864 Johnson House (Italianate); 1872 Lawrence & Chapin Iron Works (Second Empire), which started as a foundry and later housed a religious mission, skating rink, interurban station, and furniture store; 1887 turreted Michigan Central Depot (Romanesque); 1878 Wood-Upjohn House (Italianate Villa); and the 1870 Oaklands (Italianate) on the Western Michigan University campus. For a brochure, contact the Kalamazoo County Convention and Visitors Bureau, 128 N. Kalamazoo Mall, Kalamazoo MI 49007, (616) 381-4003.

Kent County

Grand Rapids. There are three walking tour routes in the Heritage Hill Historic District: Highlights include the 1910 Amberg House and 1906 Meyer May House, both designed in Prairie style by architect Frank Lloyd Wright; 1860 Philo C. Fuller House (Italianate); 1894 Deaconess House (Chateauesque), which was a school to train Methodist girls for missionary and deaconess work; 1884 Pike House (Greek Revival), which housed the Grand Rapids Art Museum from 1924 to 1980; 1883 Gay House, built on the site where Grand Rapids founder Louis Campau lived; and the 1873 Booth House (Italianate), whose 1894 garage was the first in the city built specifically for a car. For a brochure, contact the Heritage Hill Association, 126 College Ave. S.E., Grand Rapids MI 49503, (616) 459-8950.

Ottawa County

Holland. There are two walking tour routes, one focusing on the architectural and socioeconomic diversity of the city's neighborhoods, the other on its mix of commercial, religious, academic, and residential buildings. Highlights include the 1871 Hope Reformed Church (Flemish); 1927 brick Washington School; 1874 Cappon House (Italianate), built by the city's first mayor; Centennial Park; 1914 Women's Literary Club; Netherlands Museum (Classical Revival); and the 1854–56 Pillar Church, one of the largest Greek Revival churches in Michigan. For a brochure, contact the Holland Historical District Commission, City Hall, Holland MI 49423, (616) 394-1400.

CENTRAL

Bay County

Bay City's West Side. Highlights include 1860s brick Sage Mill Office on edge of Veteran's Memorial Park, built as offices for H. W. Sage & Co., a lumbering firm; O'Hare's Bar, used as a candy and cigar shop during Prohibition; 1881 Lumberman's State Bank, with the founder's monogram etched in glass on the private entrance; 1884 Sage Library (Victorian), the oldest continuously operating library in Michigan; 1891 Swart Block, with stone turret; and six houses remaining from an 1860s employee housing complex owned by Sage & Co. For a brochure, contact the Bay County Convention and Visitors Bureau, 315 14th St., Bay City MI 48708, (517) 893-1222.

Eaton County

Grand Ledge Historic District. Highlights include the 1909 Sheets-Fitzgerald House, official 1936–39 residence of Gov. Frank D. Fitzgerald and site of seances conducted by Spiritualist owners; Island Park, site of the turn-of-the-century Seven Islands Resort; 1931 brick library (Classical); 1911 Trinity Episcopal Church (Gothic Eclectic); Shane-Kimball House (Queen Anne); and the 1870s Smith Bros. Law Office (Italianate), with original crowning belvedere, formerly used as a Roman Catholic rectory. For a brochure, contact the Grand Ledge Area Historical Society, 118 W. Lincoln, Box 203, Grand Ledge MI 48837, (517) 627-3149 or 627-5170.

Ingham County

Lansing Peaks and Towers. Highlights include Victorian Eclectic homes such as 1891 Rogers-Carrier House with incised wood ornamentation in each gable; 1894 John T. Herrmann House, now used as a Lansing Community College conference center; 1878 Old Convent that formerly housed members of the Sisters of Charity; and the 1899 Harry Moore House. For a brochure, contact the City of Lansing Planning Division, 119 N. Washington Square, 2d Floor, Lansing MI 48933, (517) 483-4060.

NORTHWEST

Antrim County

Elk Rapids. Highlights include the 1901 Longfellow School; 1868 Widow Watch Inn, originally built with seven chimneys for an Episcopal rector; 1923 hydropower dam; 1860s Island House, now the public library; 1890 Carpenter Home, originally the cement works office; sites of a turn-of-the-century brewery and now-defunct iron works furnace; First Presbyterian Church, whose construction was delayed between 1873 to 1877 due to the Panic of 1873; 1900 Village Hall; and the Elk Rapids Historical Society Museum on the site of county's first log cabin. For a brochure, contact the Elk Rapids Chamber of Commerce, Box 854, Elk Rapids MI 49629, (616) 264-8202.

Muskegon County

Muskegon's Heritage Village. Highlights include the 1889 Lakeview Hotel; 1863–64 Holt House (Italianate); 1890 Montgomery House (Victorian); 1888 Hackley House (Victorian); 1894–95 C & O Union Depot (Renaissance); 1903 Emery House (Georgian Colonial Revival); 1878 Loescher House (Queen Anne); and Hackley Hose Co. No. 2, a replica nineteenth-century firebarn. For a brochure, contact the Muskegon Convention and Visitors Bureau, 349 W. Webster, Box 1087, Muskegon MI 49443-1087, (800) 235-FUNN.

Manistee County

Manistee. Highlights include the 1892 First Congregational Church (Romanesque); 1903 ornate Ramsdell Theatre, still used for community plays; 1881 Waterworks Building, now housing logging, railroad, and marine memorabilia; 1869 Our Savior Historical Church Museum, the oldest Danish Evangelical Lutheran Church in America, with Danish-style carvings; 1889 firehouse, one of the oldest continuously operating fire halls in Michigan; and the 1883 A. H. Lyman Store, now a museum and historical archive. For a brochure, contact the Manistee County Chamber of Commerce, 11 Cyprus St., Manistee MI 49660, (616) 723-2575.

UPPER PENINSULA

Chippewa County

Sault Ste. Marie Pathway to Historic Churches. Highlights include the 1902 stone St. James Episcopal Church (Gothic Revival), with 1927 Wicks pipe organ; 1902–3 sandstone First United Presbyterian Church (Romanesque), with one of the largest organs in the Upper Peninsula; 1881 brick St. Mary's Pro-Cathedral, the third church built on the site; 1932 brick St. George Greek Orthodox Church, renovated after a 1947 fire; and the 1894 red sandstone Central Methodist Church (Romanesque), listed on the National Register of Historic Places. Visitors are welcome at all the churches Sunday through Friday afternoons between 1 and 5.

For a brochure, contact the Sault Area Chamber of Commerce, 2581 I-75 Business Spur, Sault Ste. Marie MI 49783, (906) 632-3301.

Houghton County

Calumet. Highlights include the 1886 Calumet Theatre (Red Jacket Town Hall and Opera House); 1888 Union Building that housed an early bank and printing shop; 1900 sandstone St. Anne's Church (Gothic) that served the French-Canadian parishioners who supplied timber to copper mines; memorial park at the site of Italian Hall, where 73 people suffocated while fleeing a false fire alarm at a 1913 Christmas Eve party; 1898 Red Jacket firehouse of Lake Superior sandstone; 1895 Marco Curto's Saloon with original colored glass canopy; and the 1890 St. Paul the Apostle Church with Austrian stained glass windows. For a brochure, contact the Keweenaw Tourism Council, 1197 Calumet Ave., Calumet MI 49913, (906) 337-4579.

FREE VIEW: GRAND LEDGE HISTORIC DISTRICT, GRAND LEDGE

Is it only imagination, or do ghosts actually hide behind the three curtained windows on the third floor of 219 W. Jefferson St., an impressive Romanesque brick house two blocks above the Grand River? Are those birds at the feeders in the backyard or the returning spirits of departed souls?

Who knows? Now listed on the register of state historic sites, the Sheets-Fitzgerald House was built in 1907 by Spiritualists who conducted seances on the third floor, behind the three windows. I don't know what spirits appeared at those mystical gatherings, but political ghosts are certainly still here. The house served as Republican Gov. Frank D. Fitzgerald's official residence from 1935 to 1936. After a narrow reelection loss to Democrat Frank Murphy, it was here that Fitzgerald plotted his successful 1938 campaign to regain the governorship.

And it was here that he died in March 1939, only three months after his second inauguration.

Ghosts?

In *Stewards of the State*, journalist-author George Weeks gives this account of the governor's death, as told by grandson Frank M. Fitzgerald.

> Hospitalizing the governor was discussed but rejected as too alarming to the public. When a doctor, who had been summoned, rushed to his side, Fitzgerald said, "Let me up. I can't breathe." The doctor administered a heart stimulant. "Hang on, Frank," the doctor said. "We'll pull you through this one."
>
> "OK, I'll stick," the governor responded. Two minutes later he was dead.

One of the glories of a walking tour, such as the one through the Grand Ledge Historic District, is matching a site's present to its past. For example, the Italianate Smith Bros. Law Office at 207 E. Jefferson originally served as a physician's office and later became a Roman Catholic rectory.

And now-quiet Island Park, a favorite spot for ducks, was the heart of the Seven Islands Resort, a popular turn-of-the-century destination for trainloads of tourists out to enjoy steamboat rides, vaudeville theater, a boat livery, roller coaster rides, fishing, mineral wells, or a walk along the Grand River's famous sandstone ledges, or cliffs. Today, seasonal festivals are held at the park, with a paddleboat on hand to give rides on the Grand River.

We live in an age of adaptation, so it's not surprising that some historically or architecturally significant homes along the route have been converted to commercial use. A post-Victorian Princess Anne building on Taylor Street began as a private home, became a hotel, and is now used for law offices. Next door, an 1890 Carpenter Gothic house with square bay windows and elaborate exterior designs on its porches and balconies is now a dentist's office.

You don't need to know much, if anything, about architectural styles to enjoy this type of self-paced excursion, although the walking tour brochure prepared by the Grand Ledge Area Historical Society will let you sound knowledgeable enough to tell a companion, "See, that's Georgian Colonial," or "That church is obviously Eclectic Gothic."

Personally, I don't worry about the labels, preferring instead to pick out features and designs that catch my eye—belvederes and weather vanes on the roof, unusually shaped windows, ornately carved doors—and to wonder about the people who first lived in these houses or walked these sidewalks.

For me, some buildings merit only a brief glance while others provoke curiosity, questions, and reflection. What kind of shows did audiences see at the 1886 Blake's Opera House on South Bridge Street? What were the best-sellers of the day when the Ladies' Library Association opened its public library building on East Jefferson Street during the Depression?

Sheets-Fitzgerald House. (Photo by author.)

Who was invited to dance in the third-floor ballroom of the Berry-Maar House down the street from the library, and who was snubbed?
And how many other buildings have ghosts in residence?

Chapter 15

Scenic Drives

The back roads of Michigan offer thousands of miles of scenic driving and relaxed sightseeing. The contacts listed here can provide you with maps, brochures, and suggestions for places to stop along the way. Here are some recommended routes.

STATEWIDE

Cook's Tours. The state Agriculture Department has outlined more than 10 routes, each with a different agricultural theme: Michigan's Cherry Orchard in the Grand Traverse–Leelenau area, Fruit Basket along the southern Lake Michigan shore, Bean Pot in the Saginaw-Huron-Tuscola area, Sugar Bowl in the sugar beet–growing section of the Thumb, Potato Bin in the southeastern corner of the state, Apple Barrel north of Grand Rapids, Strawberry Patch on the Keweenaw Peninsula, Wine Cellar near Paw Paw, Salad Bowl southeast of Lansing, Cheese Wheel in the western Upper Peninsula, and Milk Bottle in the Sandusky-Huron-Lapeer area. Michigan Department of Agriculture Public Affairs Division, Ottawa Building North, Box 30017, Lansing MI 48909, (517) 373-1104.

Michigan Fall Tours. Enjoy seeing the fall colors? If so, the Michigan Travel Bureau has a Fall Tour brochure that suggests dozens of possible routes through prime color territory, starting in the Upper Peninsula in mid-September when the brilliant autumn colors are first evident. Michigan Travel Bureau, Box 30226, Lansing MI 48909, (800) 543-2YES.

SOUTHEAST

Chelsea Countryside. There are three routes: Valleys and Vistas, around the Waterloo Recreation Area; Steeples and Stones, through rural areas and farmland; and Pathways to the Past, along routes used by early settlers. Chelsea Area Chamber of Commerce, Box 94, Chelsea MI 48118, (313) 475-1145.

SCENIC DRIVES

SOUTHWEST

Blossom Tours. There are eight routes: Fruit Corridor Blossom, from Berrien Springs; Harbor Country Blossom, from New Buffalo; Orchard Crest Blossom, from Watervliet; Lake Country Blossom, from Dowagiac; Grapevine, from Paw Paw; Russ Forest, from Edwardsburg; Four Flags Blossom, from Niles; and Black River Blossom, from South Haven. Southwestern Michigan Tourist Council, 2300 Pipestone, Benton Harbor MI 49022, (616) 925-6301.

Battle Creek West Side. The route includes the 1910 Ralston-Purina factory; Fort Custer; Fort Custer National Cemetery; the site of Harmonia village, founded in 1844 by Spiritualists and Quakers; Kellogg Bird Sanctuary; and Leila Arboretum. Battle Creek Historic District Commission, City Hall, Box 1717, Battle Creek MI 49016, (616) 966-3320.

CENTRAL

Mecosta County Color Tour. The route includes Big Rapids, Ferris State University, Parish Fish Hatchery, Haymarsh Lake State Game Area, Chippewa Lake, School Section Lake, and Canadian Lakes. Mecosta County Convention and Visitors Bureau, 246 N. State St., Big Rapids MI 49307, (616) 796-7640 or (800) 833-6697.

NORTHEAST

River Road Scenic Byway. The route approximately parallels the Au Sable River through Iosco County in the Huron-Manistee National Forests. Sights include the U.S. Forest Service Visitor Center, with its Lumberman's Monument and Kiwanis Monument; Eagle Nest Overlook, where bald eagles nest; Iargo Springs; four hydroelectric dams; and Loud, Five Channels, Cooke, and Foote ponds. Huron-Manistee National Forests, 421 S. Mitchell St., Cadillac MI 49601, (616) 775-2421 or (800) 821-6263.

NORTHWEST

Grand Traverse Area Autumn Tour. There are five routes along the Leelanau Peninsula, Old Mission Peninsula, and Grand Traverse, Benzie, and

Antrim counties. Grand Traverse Convention and Visitors Bureau, 415 Munson Ave., Suite 200, Traverse City MI 49684, (616) 947-1120 or (800) TRAVERS.

UPPER PENINSULA

Keweenaw Waterfalls. The route takes you to 12 waterfalls, most of which are a short walking distance from the paved road. Flow is greatest in the spring, due to melting snow, but most falls have substantial flows through the summer and fall. Keweenaw Tourism Council, 326 Shelden Ave., Box 336, Houghton MI 49931, (906) 482-2388.

Mackinac Island. This is actually a bicycling or walking tour because motor vehicles are not allowed on the island. Looping the island on Lake Shore Boulevard from downtown (near Fort Mackinac) takes you past Mission Point, Arch Rock, Point Aux Pins, British Landing, Chimney Rock, Lover's Leap, and Devil's Kitchen. You also can cut across the island past the U.S. Post Cemetery, Skull Cave, and the 1814 battlefield. Mackinac Island Chamber of Commerce, Box 451, Mackinac Island MI 49757, (906) 847-3783.

Civilian Conservation Corps Sites. The U.S. Forest Service has mapped five routes to see Depression-era CCC sites. Among them are the camps where the men lived and worked and the structures they built. Highlights include nurseries, pine plantations, and fire lookout towers. Some camp buildings still stand, while at other sites all you'll find are ruins and cellar holes. Several of the camps housed German prisoners of war during World War II. Hiawatha National Forest, 2727 N. Lincoln Road, Escanaba MI 49829, (906) 786-4062.

Chapter 16

Cemeteries

It may sound morbid to some people, but Arlington National Cemetery in Virginia, Mission Dolores in San Francisco, and the Granary Burying Ground in Boston are popular tourist attractions. On your own travels through Michigan, don't be reluctant to visit a local cemetery to gain a sense of the community and a feeling for the past. In fact, far from being ghoulish or depressing, cemeteries can be fun. Some people enjoy reading tombstone inscriptions and examining the carvings on the graves. Cemeteries are places to learn about history, culture, and art, as well as places for quiet walks. If you're a bicyclist or hiker or enjoy driving along back roads and byways, you'll often come across small cemeteries—whether carefully tended or overgrown—that, by their very character, invite you to rest and explore. Detroit's Elmwood Cemetery even has a flyer listing more than 40 bird species spotted there.

Here are four suggestions.

SOUTHEAST

Detroit, Elmwood Cemetery. You'll find seven governors buried on its 83 acres, including 1848 presidential candidate Lewis Cass and William Howard, a Republican member of Congress from Detroit who served as governor of the Dakota Territory before statehood. Also here are 28 Civil War generals; 11 U.S. senators, including four who were also governors; Underground Railroad organizer William Lambert; abolitionists Joseph Ferguson and George DeBaptiste; pioneering state Geologist Douglass Houghton; 1896 Olympics wrestler Charles H. Brennan; Gen. Charles Larned, a Revolutionary War aide-de-camp to George Washington; U.S. Supreme Court Justice Henry Brown; and a slew of mayors, judges, publishers, artists, explorers, and industry magnates. For walking tour information, contact Elmwood Cemetery, 1200 Elmwood Ave., Detroit MI 48207, (313) 567-3453.

SOUTHWEST

Marshall, Oakridge Cemetery. Buried on its 65 acres are famed dime novelist William Wallace Cook; U.S. consul to the Sandwich Islands Abner Pratt; Isaac Crary, Michigan's first member of the U.S. House of Representatives; Charles Dickey, U.S. marshal and bodyguard to Abraham Lincoln; congressional chaplain Oliver Comstock; and composer Dudleigh Vernor, who wrote the music for "Sweetheart of Sigma Chi." Also buried here are three men convicted in federal court in Detroit in 1845 of helping fugitive Kentucky slave Adam Crosswhite escape on the Underground Railroad to Canada. For a cemetery walking tour map, contact the Marshall Parks, Recreation and Cemetery Department, 614 Dibble, Marshall MI 49068, (616) 781-7895.

CENTRAL

Lansing, Mt. Hope Cemetery. It includes the Monument to Unknown Firemen with a red call box marking the graves, and a 20-foot obelisk dedicated to "Our Fallen Heroes" of the Civil War. Buried here are auto pioneer Ransom E. Olds; Michigan Parks Association founder E. Genevieve Gillette; state Supreme Court Justices Edward Cahill, Russell Cowles Ostrander, and Howard Wiest; Lt. Luther Byron Baker, who captured Lincoln assassin John Wilkes Booth; and state Librarian Harriet A. Tenney. For a walking tour brochure, contact the Lansing Parks and Recreation Department, 1709 E. Mt. Hope Ave., Lansing MI 48910, (517) 483-4303.

UPPER PENINSULA

Mackinac Island, U.S. Post Cemetery. High on the center of the island are the graves of former soldiers, officers, and their families who died while a strategic military post was on the island. The identities of many of those buried here remain unknown. For information, contact the Mackinac Island Chamber of Commerce, Box 451, Mackinac Island MI 49757, (906) 847-3783.

FREE VIEW: U.S. POST CEMETERY, MACKINAC ISLAND

The dead may tell no tales, but their cemeteries do.

So it is high on the hump of Mackinac Island, between Lakes Huron and Michigan. British and American troops had vied for control of the island during the Revolution and War of 1812. Once it returned to American control, soldiers were stationed at the fort to guard the strategic Straits of Mackinac.

A white picket fence with its wooden turnstile gate surrounds rows of weathering tombstones in the U.S. Post Cemetery. Maples shade the graves and lilacs grow nearby.

These tombstones tell tales of the community on Mackinac Island, transient for the most part but dependent on each other for survival. Tens of thousands of tourists pass by this site each year on bicycle, on foot, or in horse-drawn wagons, most not bothering to stop and listen to the tales. It's reciprocal because the island's bustling fudge, T-shirt, and souvenir shops—only a few miles away—don't matter to the eternal strangers buried here.

U.S. Post Cemetery. (Courtesy Michigan Travel Bureau.)

But wandering among the graves, we wonder about the parents, wives, children, lovers, and dreams left behind when they were sent here. We wonder, too, what these strangers had thought of bitter northern winters, of life at an isolated frontier outpost, and of their futures that were not to be.

The U.S. Post Cemetery's first tale is of death far from family, far from home. "On fame's eternal camping ground, their silent tents are spread, and glory guards with solemn round, the bivouac of the dead," a memorial plaque reads.

For most of those buried here, Mackinac Island was intended as only a temporary way station, a short-term military assignment that was destined to become their permanent resting spot. Among them were such ordinary soldiers as Andrew Lawrence of Company A, 2d Infantry. Also among them were such officers as 2d Regiment Capt. John Clitz, "who died in command of this post" and was known for both "manly frankness" and for "ardent zeal and intelligence in the duties of his profession," as the broken slab marking his grave relates.

A second tale is of families. Wives and children lie here, including Mary Puthoff, "consort of Major William Puthoff"; she died on the island in 1823. Leon Rogers, 6, is buried with his father, both victims of the 1887 wreck of the *Champlain* in Lake Michigan.

The third tale is of anonymity and mystery. The identities of 70 of the 143 people buried here remain a secret more than a century old. Tombstone after tombstone is merely inscribed as "U.S. Soldier" or, more poignantly, as "Unknown U.S. Soldier." Nobody is likely to ever solve this mystery.

The U.S. Post Cemetery offers a final tale—transition. Just as these soldiers' fort is gone and their military mission is obsolete, so too will their final resting place inevitably lose the battle of permanence. The relentless weather along the Straits of Mackinac will continue to erase the inscriptions, and tombstones will continue to crack. Even so, future generations will be able to stop in the shade and, if they listen carefully, hear tales of the dead.

More to Do

Chapter 17

Ideas for Children

Of course, adults may enjoy these free opportunities too, but they have a special appeal for children.

SHIPPING LOCKS

Soo Locks, Sault Ste. Marie. It's an awesome sight to watch giant ships pass through the locks. The St. Marys River, with its rapids and 21-foot-high falls, links Lake Superior and Lake Huron. It also marks the border between Ontario and Michigan. In 1787, the Northwest Fur Co. built the first lock here, but it was destroyed during the War of 1812. Fairbanks Scale Co. built a replacement in the 1850s and turned it over to the state. Then, in 1881, the federal government took over the Soo locks.

A major transit point for shipping, the four locks average 10,000 vessels a year, ranging from small passenger boats to oceangoing freighters and tankers, some over 1,000 feet long and carrying more than 72,000 tons of cargo. One lock is named for World War II Gen. Douglas MacArthur.

The U.S. Army Corps of Engineers is responsible for the locks. There's a visitor center with a working model of a lock, a 25-minute film called "The Great Lakes Connection" on the operation and history of the locks, artifacts, photos, and a relief map of the Great Lakes. A public address system broadcasts information about downbound vessels, including tonnage, cargo, size, and nation of registry.

Outside, a fountain in the park area provides colored lights and synchronized music. Picnicking is allowed.

For more information, contact the Army Corps of Engineers, Detroit District, 477 Michigan Ave., Detroit MI 48226, (313) 226-6413.

AQUARIUM

Belle Isle Aquarium (313) 267-7159
Belle Isle Park
Detroit MI 48207

Fish, fish, and more fish beckon, along with some turtles, snakes, and other critters in the beautiful setting of Belle Isle Park. The aquarium is open daily from 10–5, with free parking in front of the building. Group guided tours can be arranged by contacting the Detroit Zoo Docent Association, Detroit Zoo, Box 39, Royal Oak MI 48068, (313) 398-0903, extension 65.

PLAYGROUNDS

If you're traveling with young children or grandchildren, a playground can be a welcome blessing. Stopping for a rest break by a school or park gives the children a chance to stretch their legs and work off pent-up energy on the swings, seesaws, slides, monkey bars, and other apparatus. Let them dig in the sandbox, get dizzy on the merry-go-round, and generally tire themselves out before a meal or the next leg of your drive.

PARADES

Who loves a parade? Just about everybody. Floats, bands, drum-and-bugle corps, clowns, fire engines, antique cars, horses, uniforms, flag corps, baton twirling, costumes, flowers, the works. And they're not limited to the Fourth of July, Memorial Day, and Labor Day. Michigan's best known parade is held in Detroit around Thanksgiving. Other communities hold them for all sorts of reasons, including festivals and the commemoration of local historical events.

FIRE STATIONS

Kids love shiny fire engines, and firefighters are often eager to show off their vehicles and equipment, explain their jobs, and answer the flood of questions kids always seem to have. It's best to call ahead and arrange a convenient time to visit.

LIBRARIES

There are more than books, magazines, and newspapers at public libraries, and you don't need to be a local resident to participate. You'll find free story hours for children, lectures and book discussions for adults, and films for all ages. Many libraries also display the work of local artists.

BOOK STORES

They want to sell books, of course, but you can enjoy hours of entertainment without cost or obligation by attending the growing number of book readings and children's story hours. Authors, well known and obscure, read from their novels, poetry, or latest nonfiction works. Some book stores also host free concerts and dance performances by local musicians and dance groups. These events are often followed by free refreshments, such as juice, coffee, and cookies.

THINKING BIG

Call them eye-openers or call them kitchy, but certainly call them noticeable.

One of Michigan's "biggest" free sights has been in Ironwood since 1964. It's hard to miss Hiawatha, billed as the "world's tallest and largest Indian." This fiberglass statue stands 52 feet tall, weighs 16,000 pounds, and can withstand 140-mph winds. It faces north toward the "Big Waters" of Lake Superior in the land of Gitchee Gummee.

Along Interstate 94 in Allen Park looms the world's largest tire, an 88-foot-high tribute to Uniroyal. From the highway, it's impossible to tell that the tire's skeleton, or framework, had been a Ferris wheel at the 1964 New York World's Fair.

CIDER MILLS

Fall in Michigan means brilliantly colored leaves, ripe apples, and fresh cider. Buying cider can make an entertaining excursion, a fun alternative to grabbing a plastic jug at the supermarket. Free activities at a cider mill can include watching the cider press operate, horse-drawn or tractor-drawn hayrides, orchard tours, festivals, farm animal petting areas for children, displays about making maple syrup and beekeeping, craft exhibits, car shows, pony rides, and live music. Many have picnic areas.

For a free directory of cider mills, farm markets, and U-pick farms, contact the Michigan Department of Agriculture, Marketing and Market Development, Ottawa Building North, Box 30017, Lansing MI 48909, (517) 373-1104.

Here's a sampling of cider mills in the state. Call ahead for hours and activities.

SOUTHEAST

Lapeer County

Apple Barn Cider Mill and Farm Market, 5404 Chapman Road, north of Lapeer, (517) 793-2853.

Lenawee County

Marvin's Fairfield Orchard, M-52, south of Adrian, (517) 436-3378.

Macomb County

Blake's Orchard and Cider Mill, 17985 Armada Center, west of Armada, (313) 784-5343.
Coon Creek Orchard and Cider Mill, 78777 Coon Creek Road, northwest of Armada, (313) 784-5062.
Stony Creek Orchard and Cider Mill, 2961 W. 32 Mile Road, west of Romeo, (313) 752-2453.
Verellen Orchards and Cider Mill, 63260 Van Dyke, south of Romeo, (313) 752-2989.

Oakland County

Diehl's Orchard and Cider Mill, 1479 Ranch Road, south of Holly, (313) 634-8981.
Yates Cider Mill, 1990 Avon Road, Rochester, (313) 651-8300.

IDEAS FOR CHILDREN

Washtenaw County

Lakeview Farm and Cider Mill, 12075 Island Lake Road, west of Dexter, (313) 426-2782.
Windy Ridge Orchard and Cider Mill, 9375 Saline-Milan Road, Saline, (313) 429-7111.

Wayne County

Davies Orchard and Cider Mill, Willow Road, south of New Boston, (313) 654-8893 or 654-6019.

SOUTHWEST

Branch County

Harrison Orchard and Cider Mill, 10250 Condit Road, south of Albion, (517) 629-6647.

Cass County

Spirit Springs Farm, Hoffman Street, south of Marcellus, (616) 646-9379.

Kent County

Bin-An-Oan Orchards, intersection of 84th Street and South Division, U.S. 131 south of Grand Rapids, (616) 455-4278 or 455-5365.
Robinette's Apple Haus and Gift Barn, 3142 4 Mile Road N.E., Grand Rapids, (616) 361-5567 or 361-7180.

CENTRAL

Barry County

Cotant's Farm Market, M-37, south of Hastings, (616) 945-4180.

Clinton County

Beck's Cider Mill, U.S. 27, north of St. Johns, (517) 224-4309.
Uncle John's Cider Mill, U.S. 27, north of St. Johns, (517) 224-3686.

Eaton County

Conklin's Cider Mill, Gresham Highway, north of Charlotte, (517) 726-0127.
Country Mill, 4648 Otto Road, Charlotte, (517) 543-1019.

Genesee County

Porter's Orchard, Farm Market, and Cider Mill, 1½ mile east of M-15, Goodrich, (313) 636-7156.

Livingston County

Spicer Orchards, Farm Market, and Cider Mill, U.S. 23, northeast of Howell, (313) 632-7692.

Montcalm County

Klackle Orchards, 11466 W. Carson City Road, west of Greenville, (616) 754-8632.

Saginaw County

Bintz Apple Farm and Cider Mill, 4535 N. River Road, northwest of Saginaw, (517) 781-2590.

NORTHEAST

Alpena County

Cripps Fruit Farm and Market, Cripps Road, southwest of Alpena, (517) 727-2005.

NORTHWEST

Grand Traverse County

Amon Orchards and Grandma's Country Market, intersection of M-72 and U.S. 31, Acme, (616) 938-9160 or (800) 937-1644.

FREE VIEW: BELLE ISLE AQUARIUM, DETROIT

How much voltage does an electric eel give off? Do piranhas savor human flesh? How do fish sleep? Does a four-eyed fish really have four eyes? Do any fish drink water?

Answers to these and other fishy questions can be found at North America's oldest public aquarium, located in the nation's largest urban island park. Opened in 1904, Belle Isle Aquarium lacks the glitz of some modern mega-aquariums, such as those in Boston and Baltimore, but it's a pleasant place to spend an hour and there's no charge for admission or parking.

There are 60 exhibits of freshwater species; saltwater exhibits were removed in 1984 because of the saltwater vapor's corrosive effects on the building. Gone since 1955 are the screened pool for sea lions and otters and the central pool for turtles and carp.

In the tanks, Great Lakes, U.S., and foreign species range from the familiar walleye, bluegill, and yellow perch to the more exotic blind cave characin of Mexico, the Malawian eye-biter, and the dwarf sting ray. Some are brilliantly colored or distinctively patterned, while others bear muted shades of brown or gray. And some boast great-sounding names, such as the kissing gourami, northern redbelly dace, quillback carpsucker, chocolate catfish, checkerboard stingray, and tiny least killifish.

You'll learn why the Australian lungfish has lungs as well as gills: lungs are essential for survival during droughts, when it burrows in the mud and must breathe air. You'll see living fossils such as the gars and lungfish with their heavy scales and dull colors, little changed by evolution over millions of years. The twig catfish is a master of camouflage, and the firewood catfish has whiskers—used for taste and touch—as long as my arm. For contrasts in size, there are tiny daphnia crustaceans and a huge alligator gar.

"This fish is not dead," explains a sign next to the sleeping goby,

Belle Isle Aquarium. (Photo by author.)

which rests on the bottom and then "springs into action" when a potential meal swims by.

In addition to the fish, the aquarium displays some reptiles and amphibians including snakes, the dinosaurlike mudpuppy, and the albino snapping turtle.

For plant lovers, next door to the aquarium is the Anna Scripps Whitcomb Conservatory, with tropical flowers, plants, and fruit trees (for more information, see chap. 4). Other free attractions in the 1,000-acre island park include playgrounds, tennis courts, walking paths, and the Dossin Great Lakes Museum.

By the way, do you know the answers to the earlier questions?

- An electric eel can give off a shock of up to 650 volts. Its "power" stuns and kills small fish for food and, like radar, helps it find its way through dark or muddy water.
- Meat-eating piranhas do have razor-sharp teeth but don't worry. They prefer prey smaller than humans. Their jaws are sometimes used as scissors in South America.
- Fish have no eyelids, so they sleep with their eyes open.
- The four-eyed fish only appears to have a double pair of eyes. In reality, it has only two, but they're subdivided horizontally. With half above the waterline and half below, it can better keep an eye out for food and predators.
- And yes, some saltwater species do drink water to help them excrete excess salt from their bodies.

Chapter 18

A Potpourri for Adults and Families

Many free activities, destinations, and attractions don't fit neatly into other categories. None of those listed in this chapter are limited to adults, but they may prove more interesting to adults and older children than to youngsters.

Here are some ideas to whet your imagination, whether you make a special trip or simply detour from your planned route.

SPECIAL BRIDGES

A boater's or canoeist's view of a bridge is far different from a motorist's perspective or that of a pedestrian or bicyclist, so any way you travel provides opportunities to appreciate them. Although Michigan has more than 11,000 bridges, here are some to keep an eye open for.

The *Blue Water Bridge,* 1.4 miles long, crosses the St. Clair River between Port Huron and Sarnia, Ontario. There's a toll for motor vehicles, but walkers can cross for free year-round.

The *Fallasburg Covered Bridge,* built of white pine in 1871, crosses the Flat River in Kent County. The original signs at the portals have been repainted, but the message is the same: "$5 Fine for Riding Or Driving On This Bridge Faster Than A Walk."

The *Siphon Bridge* in Manistique is supported in part by the Manistique River; water is atmospherically forced under it. Built in 1919, the roadway is four feet below water level.

The *Houghton-Hancock Bridge* is a double-deck lift span across the Portage Lake waterway on the Keweenaw Peninsula. It can be raised to 100 feet above the waterway, which is a canal that allows ships to take a shortcut across the peninsula. There's no toll.

The 1867 *White's Covered Bridge* in Ionia County crosses the Flat River just east of the Kent County border. It was made with hand-hewn trusses, wooden pegs, and handcut square iron nails.

The three-span *Mottville Camelback Bridge* over the St. Joseph River at Mottville is the longest existing bridge of its type. It dates from 1922.

For a free color brochure about Michigan bridges, contact the Michigan Department of Transportation, Office of Communications, Box 30050, Lansing MI 48909, (517) 335-3084.

Mackinac Bridge Walk

Since 1966, the Sunday of Labor Day weekend has meant a mass walk across the five-mile-long Mackinac Bridge, high above the Straits of Mackinac that separate the Upper and Lower peninsulas. Join 60,000–70,000 other walkers crossing free from St. Ignace at the north end to Mackinaw City to the south. Those who complete the walk get a certificate at the southern end. Arrange to be picked up in Mackinaw City or pay a small fee for a shuttle bus ride back across to St. Ignace.

For more information, contact the Mackinac Bridge Authority, Box 217, St. Ignace MI 49781, (906) 643-7600.

White's Covered Bridge. (Courtesy Michigan Department of Transportation.)

CANOE MARATHON

The annual Au Sable River Canoe Marathon has been a premier competition for more than 45 years. Each July, 25 to 30 crews from the United States and Canada take the Grayling-to-Oscoda challenge, leaving Saturday evening and arriving about 15 hours and 50,000 paddle strokes later. The event is sponsored by Au Sable River International Canoe Marathon Inc., a nonprofit group. The marathon and related weekend events draw about 40,000 spectators. It's also part of a triple crown of North American canoe racing, together with the General Clinton race in upstate New York and Le Classique marathon in Quebec.

For more information, contact the Oscoda Lodging Association, Box 165, Oscoda MI 48730, (517) 739-5156; or the Grayling Area Visitors Council, 213 James St., Grayling MI 49738, (800) 937-8837 or (517) 348-2921.

LIGHTHOUSES

Michigan boasts more than 100 lighthouses, some still active while others stand as silent sentries reminding us of the days when they were crucial to the safety of countless ships, crews, and cargoes.

Here are some you can visit free.

Lower Peninsula

Beaver Head Light is on Beaver Island in Lake Michigan. Summer visitors can climb its tower.

South Manitou Island Light, west of Leland in Lake Michigan, is in Sleeping Bear Dunes National Lakeshore and now serves as a historical museum (for more information, see chap. 1 and chap. 8).

Tawas Point Light is across Tawas Bay from Tawas City. The U.S. Coast Guard leads free tours of the lighthouse from May to November. For an appointment, contact the Coast Guard Station, 600 Lighthouse, East Tawas MI 48730, (517) 362-4428.

Upper Peninsula

Au Sable Point Light, west of Grand Marais in Pictured Rocks National Lakeshore, is open for summertime guided tours (for more information on the park, see chap. 1).

A POTPOURRI FOR ADULTS AND FAMILIES 183

Ontonagon Light is on Lake Superior near Ontonagon. To arrange a free guided tour, contact the Ontonagon County Historical Museum, 233 River St., Ontonagon MI 49953, (906) 884-6165.

Peninsula Point Light is in Hiawatha National Forest. Visitors can climb its square brick tower (for more information on Hiawatha National Forest, see chap. 5).

Point Iroquois is northwest of Brimley in Hiawatha National Forest and now houses a museum (for more information, see chap. 5 and chap. 8).

To learn more about Michigan's lighthouse legacy, contact the Great Lakes Lighthouse Keepers Association, Box 580, Allen Park MI 48101.

Au Sable Point Light. (Courtesy Michigan Travel Bureau.)

OTHER ATTRACTIONS

Sanilac Petroglyphs State Park
Greenleaf Township
Sanilac County

Neither a traditional state park nor a traditional nature preserve, Sanilac Petroglyphs is a protected archeological and anthropological treasure. Located on 238 acres of state land, these petroglyphs are the only known prehistoric carvings that survive in Michigan.

They were cut and chipped as much as 1,000 years ago into an exposed section of sandstone along the North Branch of the Cass River. Their purpose remains unknown, although they may have been carved as part of group or individual rituals, possibly related to hunting, or as part of fertility rites. They were rediscovered in the late nineteenth century. A shelter's been built over the site to protect the sensitive sandstone surface and carvings from the weather.

For more information, contact the Michigan Bureau of History, 717 W. Allegan, Lansing MI 48918, (517) 373-1668.

Veterans of Foreign Wars National Home   (517) 663-1521
3573 S. Waverly Road
Eaton Rapids MI 48827

Located on 630 acres of woods and farmland, this internationally known facility was established in 1925 for veterans' widows and orphans. It now cares for children and grandchildren of VFW and Ladies Auxiliary members. Residents live in brick houses along paved, tree-lined streets. Escorted walking tours begin with a brief overview of the campus and then cover as many as seven buildings, depending on the visitors' interests. Reservations are required.

VOLUNTEERING FOR WATER DUTY

Want to spend some free time on the water? The Traverse City–based Inland Seas Education Association seeks volunteers for its "Schoolship" program in which middle school students learn about Great Lakes ecology, history, and culture and develop an interest in active stewardship of the lakes. Half-day sessions are held aboard the 106-foot schooner

Malabar and the 114-foot schooner *Manitou*. The program covers lake biology, meteorology, geology, chemistry, physics, navigation, the arts, and culture. Students take part in such activities as trawling for fish, collecting and testing water samples, and examining plants.

Volunteers serve as instructors, working in teams for at least four days each summer. Schedules are flexible to accommodate volunteers' job and child-care needs. Prior knowledge of sailing or marine science is not necessary, and some volunteers have backgrounds as writers, teachers, or artists. They go through orientation and training sessions and will be prepared for the American Sail Training Association's level 1 deckhand and aquatic sciences certificates.

For information, contact the Inland Seas Education Association, Box 4223, Traverse City MI 49685-4223, (616) 941-5577.

RELIGIOUS SHRINES

Michigan has several internationally known religious shrines.

The *Cross in the Woods*, 7078 M-68, Indian River MI 49749, (616) 238-8973. The 55-foot redwood cross, made from the wood of a single tree, was erected on the 13-acre site in 1954. Sculptor Marshall M. Fredericks's 7-ton bronze image of Jesus was added in 1959, making this the world's largest crucifix. There's a visitor center and museum with hundreds of nun dolls dressed in the garb of their orders. Guided tours are available. Open daily from 8 A.M. to 8 P.M., April through October.

Our Lady of the Woods Shrine, Box 189, Mio MI 48647, (517) 826-5509. Dedicated in 1955, the shrine is a triangular, stone structure honeycombed with grottoes and niches. There are statues, an outdoor chapel and sanctuary, and a church. Open daily from 8 A.M. to 6 P.M., spring through fall.

Bishop Baraga Shrine, Route 2, Box 891, L'Anse MI 49946, (906) 524-7021. Known as the Shrine of the Snowshoe Priest, a brass statue by sculptor Jack Anderson honors Bishop Frederic Baraga, a Jesuit missionary called the Apostle of the Great Lakes. The Austrian-born Baraga established missions for the tribes of northern Michigan and Wisconsin. The statue is supported by five laminated wooden beams, each representing one of his major missions. The six-story-high shrine stands on a bluff overlooking Keweenaw Bay on Lake Superior. There's a visitor center. Guided tours are available. Open daily from 8 A.M. to 7 P.M., June through October.

SHOPPING MALLS

Were you born to shop? Shudder at the thought? Fall somewhere in between? Regardless, there are lots of free entertainment opportunities at shopping malls. Most popular are the shows—antiques and collectibles, RVs, arts and crafts, boats, home improvements, flowers. You'll also find art exhibits, band and choir concerts, Santa Claus, and the Easter Bunny. And you don't have to buy a thing.

COURTS

See the real world behind "Perry Mason" and "L. A. Law." The full range of human emotions and motivations is on view at civil and criminal hearings and trials in federal, state, and local courtrooms. Pick the right one and you'll find drama, suspense, mystery, and—literally—life-and-death issues.

Bishop Baraga Shrine. (Courtesy Michigan Travel Bureau.)

GALLERIES AND STUDIOS

Whether you prefer painting, sculpture, pottery, photography, textiles, handcrafted jewelry, wood carving, basketry, or another art form, there are hundreds of galleries, studios, and art fairs to visit across Michigan. Some shops are open year-round while others, particularly those in resort areas, are open only seasonally.

Some communities arrange special promotions to highlight their local studios and galleries. For example, get a free Art Craft Trails brochure covering the northwestern part of the Lower Peninsula, including the Leelanau, Traverse City, Charlevoix, Harbor Springs, and Frankfort areas from Northwestern Michigan Artists and Craftsmen, Box 92, Traverse City MI 49685. In the Lansing–East Lansing area, there's a "First Sunday" self-guided tour program of galleries, restaurants, bookstores, and craft shops on the first Sunday of each month.

ANTIQUING

It doesn't cost anything to browse through the past, and the proliferation of antique "malls" makes it even easier to find variety. Three large concentrations of antique stores and malls are found in Bay City–Saginaw, Williamston-Okemos-Mason, and Lowell–Grand Rapids.

HISTORIC MARKERS

Do you drive past those ubiquitous historical plaques with nary a glance? Next time, stop for a minute and read one. You'll find the drama of shipwrecks, fires, and war; trace the history of railroading, mining, farming, and logging; learn about Michigan's native Americans, early settlers, ethnic immigrants, and industrialists; discover more about the state's lakes, rivers, and wildlife; and read about mansions, churches, and schools. Many names you see will be unfamiliar, but you'll immediately recognize others, including inventor Thomas Edison, automaker Henry Ford, presidential candidate Thomas Dewey, Ottawa leader Chief Pontiac, magician Harry Blackstone, civil rights activist Malcolm X, cereal magnate W. K. Kellogg, and rock star Del Shannon.

Markers are erected by the Michigan Historical Commission, bar associations, local historical societies, and civic or business groups. The location and text of more than 1,000 state markers are included in *Traveling*

Through Time by Laura R. Ashlee, published by the Michigan Historical Commission.

LOG CABIN DAY

On the last Sunday of each June, dozens of log cabins and log homes across the state are open for tours and festivals, most of them free. The tradition began in 1987, during the celebration of the Michigan Sesquicentennial, the 150th anniversary of statehood. Programs vary from location to location, but often include crafts, music, and refreshments. Here are some of them.

Southeast

Port Huron. 1854 log cabin at the Museum of Arts and History, (313) 982-0891.

Southwest

Benton Harbor. 1835 Jakway Log Cabin at Sunrise Farms, (616) 944-1457.
   Cassopolis. 1923 Pioneer Log Cabin Museum, (616) 445-3087 or 445-2224.
   Grand Rapids. 1866 log cabin at Blandford Nature Center, (616) 453-6192.
   Holland. 1914 Dunningville Cabin, (616) 751-8743.
   Pearl Beach. 1830s cabin restored by Clay Township Historical Society, (313) 794-4206.

Central

Sidney. 1860 Shoen Log House at Heritage Village on Montcalm Community College campus, (517) 328-2111.

Northeast

Elkton. 1865 log cabin at Ackerman Memorial Park, (517) 375-4387.
   Gladwin. Three restored log cabins at the Gladwin County Museum, (517) 426-5562.

Parisville. 1875 log house, now the archive and library for the St. Mary's Historical Society, (517) 479-9114.

Northwest

Lake City. Late 1800s log cabin, now the Missaukee County Historical Society Museum, (616) 825-2650.

Upper Peninsula

Au Train. 1884 Paulson House at Hiawatha Folk Craft and Art Center, (906) 892-8293 or 892-8251.
Bessemer Township. 1948 cedar cabin at Eel Lake in Ottawa National Forest, (906) 932-4798.
Menominee. 1937 Michigan Department of Transportation Welcome Center, (906) 863-6496.

For more information, including a complete list of Log Cabin Day activities, contact the Log Cabin Society of Michigan, 3503 Edwards Road, Sodus MI 49126, (616) 944-5719.

FREE VIEW: MACKINAC BRIDGE WALK, ST. IGNACE

The crowd starts arriving several hours before dawn. People shiver in the almost-autumn morning darkness, stomp their feet to keep warm, and stand in sinuous, slowly moving lines to buy coffee or hot chocolate. They are waiting—for sunrise, for politicians, and for tradition.

It's Labor Day, and the advance guard of what will soon be 60,000, 70,000, or more walkers awaits the signal to cross the five-mile span of the Mackinac Bridge, the link between the Upper and Lower peninsulas. They've come by bus, car, and recreational vehicle, by bicycle or on foot for the annual Bridge Walk.

Poised at the northern end of the bridge in St. Ignace, they repeatedly check their watches. Children pull eagerly at their parents' hands, demanding to know, "Is it time yet? How much longer? When can we go?"

The governor shouts brief greetings and the surge starts, quickly enveloping, then passing, the governor, who busily waves to wellwishers and talks to news reporters as he reaches his own stride.

Mackinac Bridge Walk. (Courtesy Michigan Travel Bureau.)

The world's longest suspension bridge, Mighty Mac, welcomes its annual crowd with grace. Its huge towers dominate the scene, dwarfing the thousands of people on the roadway.

Some participants whiz along. Others amble at a more leisurely pace, perhaps leading a toddler by the hand, perhaps pushing a wheelchair or an infant in a stroller. Bicycles are not allowed.

Sunshine burns off the cold and the mist. Morning reaches into afternoon, and the crowd continues to flow southward. Many people will be met by friends and family at the end, while others will wait in lengthy queues to head back north on the shuttle bus, which charges a nominal fee.

Millions have crossed the bridge since it opened in 1957, but this once-a-year free event is a different experience from speeding across by car between the tourist communities that anchor each end. The Mackinac Bridge on foot is recreation as well as transportation, opportunity rather than expedience, a goal in itself as well as a means to an end. Walkers pause to take photos, absorb the panorama around them, or stare down through the gratings at the Straits of Mackinac, 200 feet beneath them, stretching its chilly way from Lake Michigan to Lake Huron.

This is the only time when pedestrians are welcome. As a result, it's an open-to-all gala, a massive, shared outing that began in 1966 with fewer than 100 participants but blossomed into the largest single event in the Straits area.

Here, time is more important than speed or distance. Time to look at freighters, sailboats, and yachts on the glistening water. Time to spot the distinctive, long white porch of the Grand Hotel on nearby Mackinac Island, the popular resort and tourism center that rises to the east. Time to reflect on the past, when native Americans used the Straits as a major waterway and fishing grounds, and when British and American soldiers clashed over liberty, land, and power.

There are no restrooms or food services on the bridge. If you bring children, it's a good idea to carry snacks and a water bottle in a day pack or fanny pack. You also might want a camera and binoculars.

There's no need to hurry once you reach Mackinaw City, the southern terminus. First, pick up your free official certificate of achievement to document that you completed the walk. Then stroll around the shops. Or relax on the grass, watching the bridge and its walkers, the water and the boats, and dream.

Chapter 19

Festivals

Celebrate, celebrate, celebrate. That's the theme as hometown and theme-oriented festivals proliferate across Michigan. You can have a great time even if you don't care about potatoes, blueberries, lilacs, trout, jazz, mint, or any other particular theme. And you don't have to know anybody in town to enjoy such community-oriented celebrations. No longer limited to summer weekends, hundreds of festivals are now held throughout the year.

This chapter provides a sampling of the variety of free festivals held annually. Some may impose a charge to attend specific events within the festival, however, such as concerts or dances. Food purchases are up to you.

To help plan your trips, ask the Michigan Travel Bureau for its free seasonal schedules of festivals and other tourism events. Write to Box 30225, Lansing MI 48909, or call (800) 543-2YES.

SOUTHEAST

Jackson County

Civil War Muster, Jackson. Here's a chance to see living history at the Midwest's biggest Civil War commemorative event. Hundreds of Union and Confederate "soldiers" recreate battles, drills, and military camp life. Infantry, artillery, and cavalry demonstrations are held during the annual August gathering at Cascade Falls Park. Also on the agenda are country music and bluegrass performances, a period church service, craft demonstrations, and an arts and craft show. For more information, contact Jackson County Parks, 1992 Warren Ave., Jackson MI 49203, (517) 788-4320.

Washtenaw County

Ann Arbor Art Fairs, Ann Arbor. One of the largest of all arts and craft shows, the July art fair draws more than 1,000 artists and 400,000 visitors from across the country. It's actually a combination of three simultaneous fairs—the original Ann Arbor Street Art Fair, the State Street Area Fair, and the Michigan Guild of Artists and Artisans Summer Art Fair. Events include arts and craft demonstrations, musical performances, and children's programs. For more information, contact the Ann Arbor Convention and Visitors Bureau, 211 E. Huron, Suite 6, Ann Arbor MI 48104, (313) 995-7281.

Montreux Detroit Jazz Festival. (Courtesy Lorien Studio, copyright by John Sobczak.)

Wayne County

International Freedom Festival, Detroit and Windsor. For more than three decades, this festival has been a major summer attraction with concerts, fireworks, athletic competitions, even a tug-of-war between U.S. and Canadian teams on opposite sides of the Detroit River. Known as the world's largest transborder festival, it entices more than 4.5 million people. While individual attractions vary from year to year, there's always a variety of entertainment. For more information, contact the International Freedom Festival, 100 Renaissance Center, Suite 1760, Detroit MI 48243, (313) 259-5400.

Miller Lite Montreux Detroit Jazz Festival, Detroit. The largest free jazz festival in North America includes more than 100 concerts by internationally known musicians, local artists, and high school and college musicians. Expect a wide range of sounds, including blues, bebop, Afro-Cuban, and boogie-woogie. It's held at Hart Plaza in downtown Detroit. In addition to major concerts, there are jazz clinics and club concerts during this September weekend festival, which draws as many as 750,000 fans. For more information, contact the Montreux Detroit Jazz Festival, 100 Renaissance Center, Suite 1760, Detroit MI 48243, (313) 259-5400.

Plymouth International Ice Sculpture Spectacular, Plymouth. Hundreds of thousands of pounds of block ice are transformed by carvers and culinary art students into approximately 200 sculptures that line the streets and are displayed in Kellogg Park. Indoor attractions include musical performances, art exhibits, and a gingerbread house display. There's a nighttime light show. For more information, contact the International Ice Spectacular, Box 5604, Plymouth MI 48170, (313) 459-3264.

SOUTHWEST

Berrien County

Blossomtime Festival, Benton Harbor and St. Joseph. A spring tradition for more than 80 years, 30 southwestern Michigan communities jointly celebrate the welcome season when millions of apple, peach, and other fruit trees blossom. Events include fashion shows, arts and craft shows, races, parades, and a Grand Floral Ball. For more information, contact

Tulip Time Festival. (Courtesy Tulip Time Festival Inc.)

the Blossomtime Festival, 151 E. Napier, Benton Harbor MI 49022, (616) 926-7397.

Kent County

Red Flannel Festival, Cedar Springs. Even before a red flannel factory opened here, Cedar Springs boasted how it always sold traditional long underwear—a legacy of Michigan's lumbering history, we are told. But a festival celebrating long underwear? Why not? The first Red Flannel

Day was held in 1939 and grew into an annual fall event. Activities include a marching band competition, arts and craft show, grand parade, music tent, street entertainers, old-fashioned children's games, and an antique tractor pull. "You'll find our welcome as warm as our Red Flannels," organizers boast. Of course, the Red Flannel factory outlet is open. By the way, everybody is supposed to wear red that day or risk "arrest" by the Keystone Kops. For more information, contact the Cedar Springs Area Chamber of Commerce, 66 S. Main, Box 415B, Cedar Springs MI 49319, (616) 696-3260.

Ottawa County

Tulip Time Festival, Holland. This is a big one, drawing an estimated 500,000 visitors a year to this historically Dutch community. Parades, *Klompen* dancing, Dutch attire, and tulips proliferate for the 10-day event. The festival traces its roots to 1927, when a local teacher urged the city to import 100,000 tulip bulbs, and to 1929, when concerts, a flower show, and an opera celebrated the tulips' first mass opening. For more information, contact the Tulip Time Festival, 171 Lincoln Ave., Holland MI 49423, (616) 396-4221.

U.S. Coast Guard Festival, Grand Haven. What began with a 1924 picnic expanded to festival status in 1932. That's when the Coast Guard cutter *Escanaba* was first assigned to Grand Haven, which calls itself Coast Guard City USA. Now cosponsored by neighboring Spring Lake and Ferrysburg, it attracts more than 300,000 people each year. Events include a parade, ship tours, fireworks, the world's largest musical fountain, drum and bugle corps performances, and a reunion of Coast Guard veterans. A memorial ceremony commemorates the deaths of 101 *Escanaba* crew members in a World War II torpedo attack in the North Atlantic. For more information, contact the Coast Guard Festival Committee, 41 Washington Ave., Grand Haven MI 49417, (616) 846-5940.

CENTRAL

Clinton County

Mint Festival, St. Johns. The rich black soil of Clinton County makes it the state's biggest producer of spearmint and peppermint and provides the theme for an annual summer festival. There's free entertainment, a "magnificent mint parade," craft and antique shows, mint farm tours, and a chance to meet the Mint Queen. For more information, contact the St. Johns Area Chamber of Commerce, Box 61, St. Johns MI 48879, (517) 224-7248.

Ingham County

Ag Expo, East Lansing. A 35-acre outdoor central exhibit area on the Michigan State University campus includes educational exhibits, historical displays, steam engines, and the latest in farm equipment, products, supplies, and services from 300–350 farm equipment manufacturers and suppliers. Although aimed primarily at people in farming and agribusiness, it's open to everyone. Free shuttle service is provided to daily field demonstrations. For information, contact the Agricultural Engineering Department, Michigan State University, East Lansing MI 48824-1323, (517) 355-3477.

Mecosta County

Festival of the Arts, Big Rapids. For more than 30 years, Ferris State University has sponsored a winter festival that combines the works and talents of guest artists with the school's own arts activities, including theater, music, photography, literature, and art. There are receptions, workshops, readings, lectures, concerts, exhibitions, and films. For information, contact Ferris State University, University Advancement Office, 901 S. State St., Big Rapids MI 49307-2295, (616) 592-2065.

NORTHEAST

Bay County

Fireworks Festival, Bay City. A three-day Independence Day celebration features ethnic foods, a tour of historic homes, parade, children's activities, carnival rides, and headliner entertainment. For more information, contact the Bay County Convention and Visitors Bureau, Box 2129, Bay City MI 48706, (517) 893-1222.

Potato Festival, Munger. Celebrate the spud with a parade, children's activities, old time cars, and music. It's a chance to "meat your hot potato," sponsors say. And tons of free potatoes are given away. For more information, contact the Munger Potato Festival, 1717 S. Tuscola Road, Munger MI 48747, (517) 659-2571.

Cheboygan County

Ironworkers International Festival, Mackinaw City. Begun in 1984 to commemorate the ironworkers' role in building the Mackinac Bridge, the August festival features trade skill competitions such as spud throwing, rivet catching and tossing, knot tying, rod tying, and the world-famous column climb. There's also live band music, and the Mackinac Bridge Museum is open with its videos and displays. For more information, contact the Mackinaw Area Tourist Bureau, Box 658, Mackinaw City MI 49701, (616) 436-5664 or (800) 666-0160.

Presque Isle County

Nautical City Festival, Rogers City. Here on the shore of Lake Huron, visitors will find brass bands, polka music, ethnic foods, an arts and craft show, band concerts, fire hose water fight, kiddie parade, fireworks, dancing, and a grand parade. For more information, contact the Rogers City Chamber of Commerce, Box 55, Rogers City MI 49779, (517) 734-2535 or (800) 622-4148.

NORTHWEST

Grand Traverse County

National Cherry Festival, Traverse City. One of the biggest and best known festivals in the state, the eight-day National Cherry Festival draws more than a half-million visitors each July. There are three major parades, jazz and band competitions, nonstop music on the shores of Grand Traverse Bay, sports events, and activities for children. Of course, you also get a chance to eat cherries, cherries, and more cherries in many different forms. For more information, contact the National Cherry Festival, Box 141, Traverse City MI 49685, (616) 947-4230.

Manistee County

Manistee National Forest Festival, Manistee. Lumbering helped shape this part of the state, and national forests today hold Michigan's timber resources while providing recreational opportunities. During the festival, you can see fireworks over Lake Michigan, hear concerts, tour a sawmill, and watch boats "parade" on the Manistee River. The U.S. Forest Service visitor center is open. A canoe tour of the Big Manistee River and a tour of private and national forestlands are available, as are craft and antique boat shows. For more information, contact the Manistee County Chamber of Commerce, 11 Cypress St., Manistee MI 49660, (616) 723-2575.

Newaygo County

National Baby Food Festival, Fremont. As world headquarters for Gerber Products, it's no surprise that Fremont changed its festival's name from Old-Fashioned Days to the Baby Food Festival. There are concerts, softball and basketball tournaments, kiddie and grand parades, a baby food cook-off, arts and craft show, crafts demonstrations, children's games, a baby crawl, and an antique tractor show. Gerber's visitor center is open during the festival. Naturally, there's a diaper service area—called "Rock and Rest." For more information, contact the Fremont Chamber of Commerce, 33 W. Main St., Fremont MI 49412, (616) 924-2270.

UPPER PENINSULA

Gogebic County

Pumpkin Festival, Bessemer. With Halloween ahead, the Pumpkin Festival is the place to be. Its genesis was a 1978 bet between two local residents, each of whom claimed to be able to grow the largest pumpkin. Although the first winner weighed in at only $7^1/2$ pounds, the champion so far is a 335-pound monster entered in the 1988 competition. Other events include a craft fair, retail promotions, food demonstrations, and live entertainment. There's also a children's parade and free horse-drawn wagon rides. For more information, contact the Bessemer Chamber of Commerce, Route 1, Box 25, Bessemer MI 49911, (906) 663-4542.

Tulip time in Holland. (Courtesy Tulip Time Festival Inc.)

FREE VIEW: TULIP TIME FESTIVAL, HOLLAND

Here come the *Klompen* dancers, again and again, wearing wooden shoes and Dutch ethnic attire. Here come the marching bands, again and again, with brass instruments shining and their flag corps in constant motion. Here come the antique cars, again and again, lovingly restored and polished to glisten in the late spring sun. Here come the floats, again and again, carrying costumed children, flowers, signs, even a Statue of Liberty replica and a man dressed as Abe Lincoln. And of course, here come the politicians, radio disk jockeys, and local celebrities, again and again, waving at the crowds from their convertibles.

It's May, it's Holland, it's the Tulip Time Festival, and it's the two-hour Parade of Bands.

In 1847, the Dutch settled this community on the south shore of Lake Macatawa, by Lake Michigan. The festival, more than 60 years old, reflects that Old World heritage, from the traditional scrubbing of the streets to the costumes to the 10-story windmill on Windmill Island.

It is truly a setting for the flowers that bloom in the spring, tra la. Tulips. More than 50 varieties of them. Millions of them. Brilliant combinations of reds, pinks, whites, salmons, yellows, and other hues. Proliferating in flower boxes, in manicured beds, in parks, alongside the railroad depot, and in residents' yards. Visitors can walk or drive along an eight-mile route of flower-lined Tulip Lanes.

The festival stretches over a week and a half, drawing about a half-million visitors to a combination of free and paid activities. In addition to the giant parade, free features include organ recitals at Hope College's Dimnent Chapel, authentic Dutch and early Holland church services, street scrubbing ceremonies, and a handbell concert. There's a fireworks salute and water ski show one evening. The *Klompen* dancers perform often in Centennial Park Square and in the street, and visitors at some performances are welcome to inspect their costumes.

During the festival, free art exhibits are offered at the Holland Area Arts Council downtown and at the DePree Art Center and Gallery on the Hope College campus. The Herrick Public Library displays costumes from various provinces of the Netherlands, as well as the work of local artists. A short drive from the restored nineteenth-century buildings downtown, visitors can watch artisans working at the Wooden Shoe Factory and DeKlomp Wooden Shoe and Delft Factory.

Chapter 20

Tips for Free Way Travelers

You may be on a day trip, weekend getaway, or long vacation. You may travel for pleasure or business. Whatever the circumstance or motivation, your attitude, imagination, and preparation can cut costs and open the door to memorable activities that you otherwise might miss. Here are 10 ideas to help.

1. *Ask questions.* Whether you're still in the planning stages or already on the road, ask about free or discount admission for children, students, seniors, and members of the military. Don't be embarrassed or worry about sounding cheap. Remember, members of organizations such as the American Automobile Association and the American Association of Retired Persons get reduced rates or two-for-one bargains at many tourist attractions, motels, and restaurants. Members of a museum affiliated with the Association of Science and Technology Centers get reciprocal free admission at other affiliates, including the Ann Arbor Hands-On Museum, Cranbrook Institute of Science in Bloomfield Hills, and Impression 5 Science Museum in Lansing.

2. *Use the local chamber of commerce and visitors bureau.* Before you leave or when you arrive, contact the chamber of commerce or visitors bureau for the latest listings of events, ideas for mainstream and off-the-beaten-path entertainment and recreation, and free or discount certificates. Stock up on pamphlets and maps. A list of chambers of commerce and visitors bureaus appears in the Appendix.

3. *Buy a local daily or weekly newspaper and look at bulletin boards.* These are good places to find news and schedules of upcoming cultural and community events, including library films, outdoor concerts, historical society presentations, escorted nature walks, parades, church choir performances, festivals, and other activities.

4. *Solicit suggestions from the motel desk clerk, campground manager, or bed-and-breakfast operator.* They know what's going on in their area and can give you directions. They also may have free, discount, or two-for-one coupons available.

5. *Use discount coupons.* If you intend to camp, take along grocery coupons for things you're likely to buy on the road. If you eat at restaurants, check the local newspaper for coupons and special deals, such as inexpensive, early bird menus and senior citizen discounts.

6. *Call the local high school, public library, or college.* Check with them for free concerts, arts festivals, athletic events, speakers, and other opportunities.

7. *Get free souvenirs and gifts.* Petoskey stones from Lake Michigan beaches, fossilized coral from the Lake Huron shore, and agate from Lake Superior beaches are great. Collect and press wildflowers. Consider the brochures, pamphlets, and maps you pick up as mementos of places you've been, items to keep in a scrapbook or with vacation snapshots.

8. *Remember: timing, timing, and timing. When you do things can be as important as what you do.* A few attractions, such as the Jesse Besser Museum in Alpena, offer free or discounted admission on certain days. More common are seasonal and weekend rates. Many hotels and motels that cater to business travelers and conventions during the week offer sharp discounts and special packages on weekends, often with free meals and other inducements. Tickets to some live theater performances and concerts are cheaper on weekday nights or weekend afternoons than on Friday and Saturday nights. Many movie theaters offer lower ticket prices for afternoon showings or what they call "twilight matinees," late afternoon shows that begin before 6 P.M.

9. *Be spontaneous.* Stop to listen to a street musician's impromptu performance or to speakers at a protest or political rally. Sit down to watch square dancers at the mall, Little League players on the ballfield, or hot air balloonists above your head.

10. *Be alert to free activities, even if you must pay to get in.* Visiting a state park? Some have nature centers with no extra fee and free ranger-

led programs. Touring a museum with an admission charge? Take advantage of demonstrations, presentations, and special films. Attending a concert or play? There may be a preperformance speaker or, after the performance, a chance to meet the cast. Save maps, programs, and brochures as souvenirs.

Chapter 21

Low-Cost Lodging

Lodging can prove to be the most expensive part of a trip, but there are alternatives to $100-a-night hotel rooms.

VACATION FREE

Check into the Michigan Department of Natural Resources' Campground Host Program. Applicants chosen to serve as Host Campers have free camping privileges as live-in state park and state forest hosts.

To participate, volunteers must be available for at least four weeks, generally between May 1 and September 30, and must commit themselves for five days a week, including weekends and holidays. Individuals, couples, and families may apply. Those selected bring their own accommodations, anything from a small tent to a full-size RV.

Their principal responsibility is assisting campers and other park visitors by answering questions and explaining rules. Host Campers are required to become familiar with the regulations for state parks, forests, and recreation areas, as well as with local points of interest and the location of services that visitors may ask about. Host Campers also may be asked to report emergencies, help with routine park maintenance, and assist with other campground duties, such as leading nature hikes. Due to the time commitment—about 30 hours a week—people employed more than 16 hours a week are ineligible.

Prospective Host Campers can contact the manager of the state park or state forest they're interested in. Or they can contact the Parks Division Volunteer Coordinator, Michigan State Parks, Department of Natural Resources, Box 30028, Lansing MI 48909, (517) 373-1270, or Forest Management Division, Department of Natural Resources, Box 30028, Lansing MI 48909, (517) 373-1275.

LOW-COST CAMPING

If you're used to camping at private campgrounds with amenities but not interested in free backcountry camping in the national parks (chap. 1) or national forests (chap. 5), inexpensive alternatives are the developed facilities run by federal, state, and local governments. They include more than 70 of Michigan's state parks and recreation areas, all six state forests, all three national forests, and two of Michigan's three national parks; there are no camping fees at Isle Royale National Park. In addition, many counties and municipalities have campgrounds in their own park systems. Facilities range from full hook-ups for RVs to sites without power or water connections. Some have modern toilet facilities, others don't.

HOSTELS

Despite the name, American Youth Hostels, these facilities are by no means limited to the young. It's not unusual to see families, adult travelers, and retirees take advantage of these friendly, clean, inexpensive, and relaxed accommodations. Overnight rates generally run from $5 to $15 per person, depending on location and level of services.

Unfamiliar with hostels? They offer dormitory-style accommodations, with separate quarters for males and females. There are self-service kitchens, dining areas, and common rooms. Quiet hours usually run from 11 P.M. to 7 A.M. Blankets and pillows are provided, but guests bring their own linens or rent them at the hostel; sleeping bags generally are not permitted. Guests may be asked to assist with such chores as emptying trash or sweeping the floor. No alcohol is allowed.

Many hostels now also offer rooms for families or individuals traveling together who prefer more privacy. Due to their popularity, AYH recommends reservations.

Membership in American Youth Hostels or one of its international counterparts is required. For information, contact AYH, Box 37613, Washington D.C. 20013-7613, (202) 783-6161, or the Michigan Council of AYH, 3024 Coolidge, Berkley MI 48072, (313) 545-0511.

Southeast

Country Grandma's Home Hostel (313) 753-4901
22330 Bell Road
New Boston MI 48164

Surrounded by three parks.

Heavner Home Hostel (313) 685-2379
2775 Garden Road
Milford MI 48381

Near Proud Lake State Recreation Area.

Southwest

Wabasis Lake North Country (616) 691-7260
 Hostel
11277 Springhill Drive
Greenville MI 48838

Located in a former park ranger's residence on the banks of Lake Wabasis.

Central

Mott Lake Hostel (313) 736-5760
G-6511 N. Genesee Road
Flint MI 48506

Surrounded by park land on Mott Lake.

Northwest

Brookwood Home Hostel (616) 352-4296
538 Thomas Road
Frankfort MI 49635

Overlooking Crystal Lake.

North Country Trail Association   (616) 689-6876
   Schoolhouse Hostel
3962 N. Felch
White Cloud MI 49349

Located in a refurbished schoolhouse a half-mile from the New York-to-North Dakota North Country Trail.

Upper Peninsula

Northstar Home Hostel   (906) 249-3085
545 Lakewood Lane
Marquette MI 49855

Overlooking Lake Superior.

HEAD FOR CAMPUS

Some Michigan colleges and universities make dormitory rooms available to the general public—people who are not on campus for college-related events or conventions and are not necessarily related to students.

Such facilities are generally available during school vacations. Accommodations aren't plush but are inexpensive, clean, and safe. Televisions are generally found in lounges rather than individual rooms or suites. Rates for a double room range from $8–25 plus tax. At some schools, guests must provide their own linens. Guests are often entitled to use cafeterias, athletic, and other facilities.

College policy often prohibits alcohol in the dorms, even for guests 21 and older.

Codes are Y (yes) and N (no) for Pets / Children / Private Bath / Room Phone / Linens / Cooking / Free parking.

Southwest

Grace Bible College   (616) 538-2330   N Y N N N N Y
Business Office
1011 Aldon S.W.
Box 910
Wyoming MI 49509

Available May 15–August 15. Reservations required 1 week in advance. Five-guest minimum. No alcohol. Accepts credit cards, personal checks, travelers checks, or cash.

Central

Ferris State University   (616) 592-3745   N Y Y Y Y N Y
Residential Life Office
901 S. State
Big Rapids MI 49307

Available June 8–August 25. Reservations not required. Alcohol only in rooms. Accepts personal checks, travelers checks, or cash.

Northwood Institute   (517) 837-4375   N Y Y Y Y N Y
Housing Department
3225 Cook Road
Midland MI 48640

Available June 15–August 20. Reservations required six weeks in advance. Three guests maximum per suite, but apartments also are available. No alcohol. Cash only.

Northwest

North Central Michigan College Conference and Food Service Office 1515 Howard St. Petoskey MI 49770	(616) 348-6612 or 348-6611	N	Y	Y	Y	Y	N	Y

Available year-round. Reservations required at least two weeks in advance. Travelers checks, personal checks, or cash.

Appendix: Travel and Recreation Information Sources

When planning your travel and recreational activities, regional and local tourist and convention bureaus and chambers of commerce are valuable sources of free information, including brochures, maps, special events schedules, and lists of accommodations. Some have toll-free telephone numbers.

STATEWIDE

Michigan Travel Bureau (800) 543-2YES
Box 30226
Lansing MI 48909

REGIONAL

Eastern Upper Peninsula Tourist Association (906) 643-7343
100 Marley
County Courthouse
St. Ignace MI 49781

Metropolitan Detroit Convention (313) 259-4333
and Visitors Bureau
100 Renaissance Center, Suite 1950
Detroit MI 48234

Greater Detroit Chamber of Commerce (313) 964-4000
600 W. Lafayette Blvd.
Detroit MI 48826

Southwestern Michigan Tourist Council (616) 925-6301
c/o Howard Johnson's
2699 M-139
Benton Harbor MI 49022

Upper Peninsula Travel and Recreation Association (800) 562-7134
Box 400 (906) 774-5480
Iron Mountain MI 49801

West Michigan Tourist Association (616) 456-8557
136 E. Fulton St.
Grand Rapids MI 49503

LOCAL

Greater Albion Chamber of Commerce (517) 629-5533
300 N. Eaton St.
Albion MI 49224

Alger County Chamber of Commerce (906) 387-2138
Box 405
Munising MI 49862

Greater Algonac Chamber of Commerce (313) 794-5511
Box 363
Algonac MI 48001

Allegan Area Chamber of Commerce (616) 673-2479
Box 338
Allegan MI 49010

Allen Park Chamber of Commerce (313) 382-7303
6601 Park Ave.
Allen Park MI 48101

Alma Chamber of Commerce (517) 463-5525
1110 W. Superior
Alma MI 48801

Alpena Area Chamber of Commerce (800) 582-1906
133 Johnson St. (517) 354-4181
Alpena MI 49707

Anchor Bay Chamber of Commerce (313) 949-4120
Box 22
New Baltimore MI 48047

Ann Arbor Convention and Visitors Bureau (313) 995-7281
211 E. Huron, Suite 6
Ann Arbor MI 48104

Atlanta Area Chamber of Commerce (517) 785-3400
Box 410
Atlanta MI 49709

Auburn Area Chamber of Commerce (517) 662-4408
Box 215
Auburn MI 48611

Auburn Hills Chamber of Commerce (313) 335-9695
64 N. Saginaw St., Suite 101B
Pontiac MI 48342

AuGres Chamber of Commerce (517) 876-6688
Box 455
AuGres MI 48703

Bad Axe Chamber of Commerce (517) 269-7661
Box 87
Bad Axe MI 48413

Baraga County Tourist and Recreation Association (906) 524-7444
Box 556
Baraga MI 49908

Battle Creek Area Visitors and Convention Bureau (616) 962-2240
34 W. Jackson St., Suite 4-B
Battle Creek MI 49017

Bay County Convention and Visitors Bureau   (517) 893-1222
Box 2129
Bay City MI 48706

Belding Area Chamber of Commerce   (616) 794-2210
120 Covered Village
Belding MI 48809

Bellaire Chamber of Commerce   (616) 533-6023
Box 205
Bellaire MI 49615

Belleville Area Chamber of Commerce   (313) 697-7151
116 Fourth St.
Belleville MI 48111

Bellevue Chamber of Commerce   (616) 763-9403
218 S. Main St.
Bellevue MI 49021

Benzie County Chamber of Commerce   (616) 882-5801
Box 505
Beulah MI 49617

Greater Berkley Chamber of Commerce   (313) 544-9464
Box 1253
Berkley MI 48072

Berrien Springs/Eau Claire Chamber of Commerce   (616) 471-2351
Box 222
Berrien Springs MI 49103

Bessemer Chamber of Commerce   (906) 663-4542
Rte. 1, Box 25
Bessemer MI 49911

Birmingham/Bloomfield Chamber of Commerce   (313) 644-1700
240 Martin St.
Birmingham MI 48009

Blissfield Chamber of Commerce (517) 486-3836
Box 25
Blissfield MI 49228

Blue Water Area Tourist Bureau (800) 852-4242
520 Thomas Edison Parkway (313) 987-8687
Port Huron MI 48060

Boyne City Chamber of Commerce (616) 582-6222
28 S. Lake
Boyne City MI 49712

Boyne Country Convention and Visitors Bureau (800) 872-8377
Box 694 (616) 348-2755
Petoskey MI 49770

Bridgeport Area Chamber of Commerce (517) 777-9180
Box 387
Bridgeport MI 48722

Greater Brighton Area Chamber of Commerce (313) 227-5086
131 Hyne St.
Brighton MI 48116

Bronson Chamber of Commerce (517) 369-1110
Box 152
Bronson MI 49028

Brooklyn/Irish Hills Chamber of Commerce (517) 592-8907
106 Main St.
Brooklyn MI 49230

Buchanan Area Chamber of Commerce (616) 695-3291
119 Main St.
Buchanan MI 49107

Burr Oak Chamber of Commerce (616) 489-5075
Box 308
Burr Oak MI 49030

Cadillac Area Visitors Bureau (800) 225-2537
222 Lake St. (616) 775-9776
Cadillac MI 49601

Canton Chamber of Commerce (313) 453-4040
44968 Ford Road, Suite K
Canton MI 48187

Capac Area Chamber of Commerce (313) 395-2243
Box 386
Capac MI 48014

Caro Area Chamber of Commerce (517) 673-5211
121 N. State, Suite 2
Caro MI 48723

Carson City Area Chamber of Commerce (517) 584-6543
Box 18
Carson City MI 48811

Cassopolis Area Chamber of Commerce (616) 445-2891
Box 154
Cassopolis MI 49031

Cedar Springs Area Chamber of Commerce (616) 696-3260
Box 415
Cedar Springs MI 49319

Central Lake Chamber of Commerce (616) 544-3322
Box 428
Central Lake MI 49622

Central Macomb County Chamber of Commerce (313) 463-1528
58 North Ave.
Mt. Clemens MI 48043

Charlevoix Area Convention and Visitors Bureau (800) 367-8557
408 Bridge St. (616) 547-2101
Charlevoix MI 49720

Charlotte Chamber of Commerce (517) 543-0400
207 S. Cochran Ave.
Charlotte MI 48813

Cheboygan Area Tourist Bureau (616) 627-7183
Box 69
Cheboygan MI 49721-0069

Chelsea Area Chamber of Commerce (313) 475-1145
Box 94
Chelsea MI 48118

Chesaning Chamber of Commerce (517) 845-3055
220 E. Broad St.
Chesaning MI 48616

Clare Area Chamber of Commerce (517) 386-2442
609 McEwan
Clare MI 48617

Clarkston Chamber of Commerce (313) 625-8055
Box 938
Clarkston MI 48347

Clawson Chamber of Commerce (313) 435-2450
615 N. Main St.
Clawson MI 48017

Coldwater/Branch County Chamber of Commerce (517) 278-5985
20 Division St.
Coldwater MI 49036

Coloma Area Chamber of Commerce (616) 468-3377
Box 418
Coloma MI 49038

Coopersville Area Chamber of Commerce (616) 837-9731
289 Danforth St.
Coopersville MI 49404

Davison Area Chamber of Commerce (313) 653-6266
102 E. Second St.
Davison MI 48423

Dearborn Chamber of Commerce (313) 584-6100
15544 Michigan Ave.
Dearborn MI 48126

Dearborn Heights Chamber of Commerce (313) 274-7480
24624 W. Warren
Dearborn Heights MI 48127

Delta County Tourist and Recreation Bureau (906) 786-2192
230 Ludington St.
Escanaba MI 49829-4098

Dickinson County Tourism Association (906) 774-2002
Box 672
Iron Mountain MI 49801

Greater Dowagiac Chamber of Commerce (616) 782-8212
107 Beeson St.
Dowagiac MI 49047

Greater Durand Area Chamber of Commerce (517) 288-3715
100 W. Clinton St.
Durand MI 48429

East Jordan Chamber of Commerce (616) 536-7351
Box 137
East Jordan MI 49727

Eastpointe Chamber of Commerce (313) 776-5520
Box 24
Eastpointe MI 48021-2389

Edmore Area Chamber of Commerce (313) 427-5821
Box 103
Edmore MI 48829

Edwardsburg Chamber of Commerce (616) 663-2756
Box 575
Edwardsburg MI 49112

Elberta Chamber of Commerce (616) 352-9264
Box 337
Elberta MI 49628

Elk Rapids Area Chamber of Commerce (616) 264-8202
Box 854
Elk Rapids MI 49629

Evart Area Chamber of Commerce (616) 734-5594
129 N. Main St.
Evart MI 49631

Farmington/Farmington Hills Chamber of Commerce (313) 474-3440
33411 Grand River Ave.
Farmington MI 48335-3521

Fennville Area Chamber of Commerce (616) 561-5013
Box 484
Fennville MI 49408

Fenton Area Chamber of Commerce (313) 629-5447
207 Silver Lake Road
Fenton MI 48430

Ferndale Chamber of Commerce (313) 542-2160
400 E. Nine Mile Road
Ferndale MI 48220

Fife Lake Chamber of Commerce (616) 879-4471
Box 117
Fife Lake MI 48633

Flint Area Convention and Visitors Bureau (800) 288-8040
400 N. Saginaw St., Suite 101A (313) 232-8900
Flint MI 48502

Flushing Area Chamber of Commerce (313) 659-4141
Box 44
Flushing MI 48433

Four Flags Area Council on Tourism (616) 683-3720
321 E. Main St.
Box 10
Niles MI 49120-3720

Frankenmuth Convention and Visitors Bureau (517) 652-6106
635 S. Main St.
Frankenmuth MI 48734

Freeland Area Chamber of Commerce (517) 695-6620
Box 484
Freeland MI 48623

Fremont Chamber of Commerce (616) 924-0770
33 W. Main St.
Fremont MI 49412

Garden City Chamber of Commerce (313) 422-4448
30120 Ford Road, Suite D
Garden City MI 48135

Gaylord/Otsego County Convention and (517) 732-4000
   Tourist Bureau
125 S. Otsego
Gaylord MI 49735

Gladwin County Chamber of Commerce (517) 426-5451
608 W. Cedar
Gladwin MI 48624

Gogebic Area Convention and Visitors Bureau (800) 272-7000
Box 706 (906) 932-4850
Ironwood MI 49938

Grand Blanc Chamber of Commerce (313) 695-4222
131 E. Grand Blanc Road
Grand Blanc MI 48439

Grand Haven/Spring Lake Area Visitors Bureau (616) 842-4499
1 South Harbor Dr.
Grand Haven MI 49417

Grand Ledge Area Chamber of Commerce (517) 627-2383
Box 105
Grand Ledge MI 48837-0105

Grand Rapids Area Convention and Visitors Bureau (800) 678-9859
245 Monroe N.W. (616) 459-8287
Grand Rapids MI 49503

Greater Grandville Chamber of Commerce (616) 531-8890
2905 Wilson Ave., Suite 101A
Grandville MI 49468-0175

Grand Traverse Convention and Visitors Bureau (800) 872-8377
415 Munson Ave., Suite 200 (616) 947-1120
Traverse City MI 49684

Grayling Area Visitors Council (800) 937-8837
213 James St. (517) 348-2921
Grayling MI 49738

Greenbush Chamber of Commerce (517) 739-7635
4115 S. U.S. 23
Greenbush MI 48838

Greenville Area Chamber of Commerce (616) 754-5697
202 S. Lafayette St.
Greenville MI 48838

Gun Lake Area Chamber of Commerce (616) 672-7822
77 124th Ave.
Shelbyville MI 49344

Hale Area Chamber of Commerce (800) 722-8229
Box 68
Hale MI 48739

Hamtramck Chamber of Commerce (313) 875-7877
9435 Joseph Campau
Hamtramck MI 48212

Harbor Beach Chamber of Commerce (517) 479-6450
149 N. Fourth St.
Harbor Beach MI 48441

Harbor Country Chamber of Commerce (616) 469-5409
3 W. Buffalo
New Buffalo MI 49117-0497

Harbor Springs Chamber of Commerce (616) 347-4150
Box 37
Harbor Springs MI 49740

Harrison Area Chamber of Commerce (517) 539-6011
809 N. First
Harrison MI 48625

Hart-Silver Lake Chamber of Commerce (616) 873-2247
Box 69
Hart MI 49420

Hastings Area Chamber of Commerce (616) 945-2454
Box 236
Hastings MI 49058

Hazel Park Chamber of Commerce (313) 543-8556
Box 85
Hazel Park MI 48030

Hesperia Area Chamber of Commerce (616) 854-1080
Box 32
Hesperia MI 49421-0032

Highland Park Chamber of Commerce (313) 868-6420
12541 Second Ave.
Highland Park MI 48203

Hillman Area Chamber of Commerce (517) 742-3739
Box 506
Hillman MI 49746

Greater Hillsdale Chamber of Commerce (517) 439-4341
49 S. Howell St.
Hillsdale MI 49242

Holland Area Convention and Visitors Bureau (800) 822-2770
171 Lincoln Ave. (616) 396-4221
Holland MI 49423

Holly Area Chamber of Commerce (313) 634-1900
102 Civic Drive
Holly MI 48442

Houghton Lake Chamber of Commerce (800) 292-9071
1625 W. Houghton Lake Drive (517) 366-5644
Houghton Lake MI 48269

Howell Area Chamber of Commerce (517) 546-3920
404 E. Grand River Ave.
Howell MI 48843

Hudson Area Chamber of Commerce (517) 448-8983
Box 45
Hudson MI 49247

Hudsonville Chamber of Commerce (616) 896-9020
Box 216
Hudsonville MI 49426

Huron County Tourist Association (517) 269-8463
Huron County Building
Bad Axe MI 48413

Huron Shores Chamber of Commerce (517) 724-5107
Box 151
Harrisville MI 48740

Huron Township Chamber of Commerce (313) 753-4220
19132 Huron River Drive
New Boston MI 48164

Huron Valley Area Chamber of Commerce (313) 685-7129
371 N. Main
Milford MI 48381

Imlay City Area Chamber of Commerce (313) 724-1361
Box 206
Imlay City MI 48444

Indian River Resort Region Chamber of Commerce (616) 238-9325
Box 57
Indian River MI 49749

Inkster Chamber of Commerce (313) 225-0450
26700 Princeton
Inkster MI 48141

Interlochen Chamber of Commerce (616) 276-7141
Box 13
Interlochen MI 49643

Ionia Area Chamber of Commerce (616) 527-2560
428 W. Washington St.
Ionia MI 48846

Iron County Tourism Council (906) 265-3822
1 E. Genesee
Iron River MI 49935

Ironwood Tourism Council (906) 932-1122
100 E. Aurora St.
Ironwood MI 49938

Isabella County Convention and Visitors Bureau (800) 772-4433
210 E. Broadway (517) 772-4433
Mt. Pleasant MI 48858

Greater Ishpeming Chamber of Commerce (906) 486-4841
661 Palms Ave.
Ishpeming MI 49849

Ithaca Chamber of Commerce (517) 875-3640
Box 44
Ithaca MI 48847

Jackson Convention and Tourist Bureau (800) 245-5282
109 W. Washington (517) 783-3330
Jackson MI 49201

Jennison Chamber of Commerce
Box 405
Jennison MI 49428

Kalamazoo County Convention and Visitors Bureau (616) 381-4003
128 N. Kalamazoo Mall
Kalamazoo MI 49005

Greater Kalkaska Area Chamber of Commerce (616) 258-9103
350 S. Cedar St.
Kalkaska MI 49646-0291

Keweenaw Tourism Council (800) 338-7982
Box 336 (906) 482-2388
Houghton MI 49931

Lake City Area Chamber of Commerce (616) 745-4331
229 S. Main
Lake City MI 49651

Lake County Chamber of Commerce (616) 745-4331
Box 130
Baldwin MI 49304

Lake Gogebic Area Chamber of Commerce (906) 575-3265
Box 114-B
Bergland MI 49910

Lakes Area Chamber of Commerce (313) 624-2826
8585 PGA Drive, Suite 102
Walled Lake MI 48390

Lakeshore Convention and Visitors Bureau (616) 637-5252
567 Dyckman
Box 28
South Haven MI 49090

Greater Lansing Convention and Visitors Bureau (517) 487-6800
119 Pere Marquette
Box 15066
Lansing MI 48901-5066

Lapeer Area Chamber of Commerce (313) 664-6641
446 Pine St.
Lapeer MI 48446

Leelanau County Chamber of Commerce (616) 256-9895
Box 212
Lake Leelanau MI 49653

Lenawee County Chamber of Commerce (517) 265-5141
216 N. Main St.
Adrian MI 49221

LeRoy Chamber of Commerce (616) 768-4443
104 Underwood
LeRoy MI 49655

Les Cheneaux Chamber of Commerce (906) 484-3935
Box 10
Cedarville MI 49719

Lewiston Area Chamber of Commerce (517) 786-2293
Box 656
Lewiston MI 49756

Lexington Chamber of Commerce (313) 359-2262
Box 142
Lexington MI 48450

Lincoln Park Chamber of Commerce (313) 386-0140
3014 Fort St.
Lincoln Park MI 48146

Linden/Argentine Chamber of Commerce (313) 750-8794
Box 565
Linden MI 48451

Litchfield Chamber of Commerce (517) 542-2351
Box 343
Litchfield MI 49252

Livonia Chamber of Commerce (313) 427-2122
15401 Farmington Road
Livonia MI 48154-2892

Lowell Area Chamber of Commerce (616) 897-9161
Box 224
Lowell MI 49331

Ludington Area Convention and Visitors Bureau (800) 542-4600
5827 W. U.S. 10 (616) 845-0324
Box 160
Ludington MI 49431

Mackinaw Area Tourist Bureau (800) 666-0160
Box 658 (616) 436-5664
Mackinaw City MI 49701

Mackinac Island Chamber of Commerce (906) 847-3783
Box 451
Mackinac Island MI 49757

Madison Heights Chamber of Commerce (313) 542-5010
26385 John R
Madison Heights MI 48701

Manchester Chamber of Commerce (313) 428-7722
Box 433
Manchester MI 48158

Manistee County Chamber of Commerce (616) 723-2575
11 Cypress St.
Manistee MI 49660

Manistique Area Chamber of Commerce (906) 341-8433
Box 72
Manistique MI 49854

Marine City Chamber of Commerce (313) 765-4501
515 S. Parker, Suite G
Marine City MI 48039

Marion Chamber of Commerce (616) 743-2461
Box 279
Marion MI 49665

Marlette Area Chamber of Commerce (517) 635-2429
Box 222
Marlette MI 48453

Marquette County Tourism Council (800) 544-4321
501 S. Front St. (906) 228-7740
Marquette MI 49855

Marshall Area Chamber of Commerce (616) 781-5163
109 E. Michigan Ave.
Marshall MI 49068

Marysville Area Chamber of Commerce (313) 364-6180
2827 Gratiot Blvd., Suite 3
Marysville MI 48040

Mason Area Chamber of Commerce (517) 676-1046
148 E. Ash St.
Mason MI 48854

McBain Area Chamber of Commerce (616) 825-2416
Box 53
McBain MI 49657

Mecosta County Convention and Visitors Bureau (800) 833-6697
246 N. State St. (616) 796-7640
Big Rapids MI 49307

Menominee Area Chamber of Commerce (906) 863-2679
1005 Tenth Ave.
Menominee MI 49858

Metro East Chamber of Commerce (313) 777-2741
27601 Jefferson Ave.
St. Clair Shores MI 48081-2053

Midland County Convention and Visitors Bureau (800) 678-1961
300 Rodd St. (517) 839-9901
Midland MI 48640

Monroe County Convention and Tourist Bureau (800) 252-3011
Box 1094 (313) 242-3366
Monroe MI 48161

Montrose Area Chamber of Commerce (313) 639-3475
Box 628
Montrose MI 48457

Mt. Pleasant Area Chamber of Commerce (517) 772-2396
210 E. Broadway
Mt. Pleasant MI 48858

Munising Visitors Bureau (906) 387-4864
Box 310
Munising MI 49862

Muskegon County Convention and Visitors Bureau (800) 235-3866
349 W. Webster Ave. (616) 722-3751
Muskegon MI 49440

Nashville Chamber of Commerce (517) 852-9593
311 N. State St.
Nashville MI 49073

Newaygo Chamber of Commerce (616) 652-3068
330 Adams St.
Newaygo MI 49337

Newberry Chamber of Commerce (906) 293-5562
Box 308
Newberry MI 49868

Northville Community Chamber of Commerce (313) 349-7640
195 S. Main St.
Northville MI 48167

Novi Chamber of Commerce (313) 349-3743
25974 Novi Road
Novi MI 48375

Oakland County Chamber of Commerce (313) 688-4747
1052 W. Huron St.
Waterford MI 48328

Onaway Chamber of Commerce (517) 733-6620
310 W. State St.
Onaway MI 49765

Ontonagon Tourism Council (906) 884-4735
Box 266
Ontonagon MI 49953

Orion Area Chamber of Commerce (313) 693-9300
Box 236
Lake Orion MI 48361-0236

Greater Ortonville Chamber of Commerce (313) 627-2811
Box 152
Ortonville MI 48462

Oscoda/Au Sable Chamber of Commerce (517) 739-7322
100 W. Michigan
Oscoda MI 48750

Oscoda Lodging Association (517) 739-5156
Box 165
Oscoda MI 48750

Otsego Chamber of Commerce (616) 694-6880
100 W. Allegan St.
Otsego MI 49078

Ottawa County Association of Commerce and Industry (616) 842-4910
1 South Harbor Drive
Grand Haven MI 49417

Owosso-Corunna Area Chamber of Commerce (517) 723-5149
215 N. Water St.
Owosso MI 48867

Oxford Area Chamber of Commerce (313) 628-4691
Box 142
Oxford MI 48051

Paradise Area Tourism Council (906) 492-3927
Box 64
Paradise MI 49768

Greater Paw Paw Chamber of Commerce (616) 657-5395
Box 105
Paw Paw MI 49079

Pentwater Area Chamber of Commerce (616) 869-4150
Box 614
Pentwater MI 49449

Petoskey Regional Chamber of Commerce (616) 347-4150
401 E. Mitchell
Petoskey MI 49770

Pigeon Chamber of Commerce (517) 453-2506
Box 618
Pigeon MI 48755

Pinconning Area Chamber of Commerce (517) 879-2816
Box 856
Pinconning MI 48650

Plainwell Chamber of Commerce (616) 685-8877
Box 95
Plainwell MI 49080

Plymouth Community Chamber of Commerce (313) 453-1540
386 S. Main St.
Plymouth MI 48170

Pontiac Chamber of Commerce (313) 335-9600
64 N. Saginaw St., Suite 101B
Pontiac MI 48342

Greater Port Huron/Marysville Chamber of Commerce (313) 985-7101
920 Pine Grove Ave.
Port Huron MI 48060

Greater Port Sanilac Business Association
Box 402
Port Sanilac MI 48469

Portland Area Chamber of Commerce (517) 647-2100
1327 Grand River Ave.
Portland MI 48875

Quincy Chamber of Commerce (517) 639-3115
Box 4
Quincy MI 49082

Ravenna Chamber of Commerce (616) 853-2190
Box 177
Ravenna MI 49451

Redford Township Chamber of Commerce (313) 535-0960
26050 Five Mile
Redford MI 48239

Reed City Area Chamber of Commerce (616) 832-5431
Box 27
Reed City MI 49677

Reese Chamber of Commerce (517) 776-7525
12880 Washington
Reese MI 48757

Richmond Chamber of Commerce (313) 727-7581
Security Bank Building
Richmond MI 48062

River Country Tourism Council (616) 467-4505
150 N. Main St.
Box 70
Centreville MI 49032

Greater Rochester Area Chamber of Commerce (313) 651-6700
71 Walnut, Suite 110
Rochester MI 48307

Rockford Area Chamber of Commerce (616) 866-2000
Box 520
Rockford MI 49341

Rogers City Chamber of Commerce (517) 734-2535
Box 55
Rogers City MI 49779

Romeo-Washington Chamber of Commerce (313) 752-4436
Box 175
Romeo MI 48065

Greater Romulus Chamber of Commerce (313) 326-4290
31200 Detroit Industrial Expressway
Romulus MI 48174

Greater Royal Oak Chamber of Commerce (313) 547-4000
411 S. Lafayette
Royal Oak MI 48067

Saginaw County Convention and Visitors Bureau (800) 444-9979
901 S. Washington (517) 752-7164
Saginaw MI 48601

St. Charles Area Chamber of Commerce (517) 865-8287
110 W. Spruce
St. Charles MI 48655

St. Helen Chamber of Commerce (517) 389-3725
Box 642
St. Helen MI 48656

St. Ignace Area Tourism Association (800) 643-8717
11 S. State St. (906) 643-6950
St. Ignace MI 49781

St. Johns Area Chamber of Commerce (517) 224-7248
Box 61
St. Johns MI 48879

St. Louis Area Chamber of Commerce (517) 681-3825
Box 161
St. Louis MI 48880

Saline Area Chamber of Commerce (313) 429-4494
107 1/2 E. Michigan Ave.
Saline MI 48176

Greater Sandusky Area Chamber of Commerce (313) 648-4445
26 W. Speaker
Sandusky MI 48471

Sanford Area Chamber of Commerce (517) 687-2800
Box 98
Sanford MI 48657

Saugatuck/Douglas Convention and Visitors Bureau (616) 857-5801
Box 28
Saugatuck MI 49453

Sault Ste. Marie Tourism Bureau (800) 647-2858
2581 I-75 Business Spur (906) 632-3301
Sault Ste. Marie MI 49783

Schoolcraft County Chamber of Commerce (906) 341-5010
Box 72
Manistique MI 49854

Scottville Chamber of Commerce (616) 757-3301
133 S. Main
Scottville MI 49454

Sebewaing Chamber of Commerce (517) 883-2150
108 W. Main St.
Sebewaing MI 48759

Shelby Chamber of Commerce (616) 861-4054
Box 193
Shelby MI 49455

Shepherd Area Chamber of Commerce (517) 828-6683
Box 111
Shepherd MI 48883-0111

Skidway Lake Area Chamber of Commerce   (517) 873-4150
2777 Greenwood Road
Prescott MI 48756-4041

Greater South Haven Area Chamber of Commerce   (616) 637-5171
535 Quaker St.
South Haven MI 49090

South Lyon Area Chamber of Commerce   (313) 437-3257
214 S. Lafayette
South Lyon MI 48178

Southern Wayne County Chamber of Commerce   (313) 284-6000
20600 Eureka, Suite 315
Taylor MI 48180

Southfield Chamber of Commerce   (313) 557-6400
16250 Northland Drive, Suite 130
Southfield MI 48075

Standish Chamber of Commerce   (517) 846-7867
Box 458
Standish MI 48658

Sterling Heights Area Chamber of Commerce   (313) 731-5400
12900 Hall Road, Suite 110
Sterling Heights MI 48313

Sturgis Area Chamber of Commerce   (616) 651-5758
200 W. Main
Sturgis MI 49091

Suttons Bay Chamber of Commerce   (616) 256-9895
Box 212
Lake Leelanau MI 49653

Swartz Creek Area Chamber of Commerce   (313) 635-9643
Box 267
Swartz Creek MI 48473

Tawas Bay Tourist Bureau (800) 448-2927
Box 10 (517) 362-8643
Tawas City MI 48764

Tecumseh Chamber of Commerce (517) 423-3740
101 W. Chicago Blvd.
Tecumseh MI 49286

Three Rivers Area Chamber of Commerce (616) 278-8193
140 W. Michigan Ave.
Three Rivers MI 49093

Thunder Bay Regional Convention (800) 582-1906
   and Visitors Bureau (517) 354-4181
Box 65
Alpena MI 49707

Traverse City Area Chamber of Commerce (616) 947-5075
202 E. Grandview Parkway
Traverse City MI 49685-0387

Troy Chamber of Commerce (313) 641-8151
4555 Corporate Drive, Suite 300
Troy MI 48098

Trufant Area Chamber of Commerce (616) 984-2153
Box 2
Trufant MI 49347

Twin Cities Area Chamber of Commerce (616) 925-0044
Box 1208
Benton Harbor MI 49023-1208

Vassar Chamber of Commerce (517) 823-2601
Box 126
Vassar MI 48768

Warren/Center Line/Sterling Heights Chamber of Commerce
30500 Van Dyke, Suite 118
Warren MI 48093
(313) 751-3939

Wayland Chamber of Commerce
160 W. Superior
Wayland MI 49348
(616) 792-2265

Wayne Chamber of Commerce
35816 W. Michigan Ave.
Wayne MI 48184
(313) 721-0359

West Bloomfield Chamber of Commerce
6668 Orchard Lake, Suite 209
West Bloomfield MI 48322
(313) 626-3636

West Branch/Ogemaw County Travel and Visitors Bureau
422 W. Houghton Ave.
West Branch MI 48661
(517) 345-2821

Westland Chamber of Commerce
36900 Ford Road
Westland MI 48185
(313) 326-7222

White Cloud Chamber of Commerce
Box 158
White Cloud MI 49349
(616) 689-6607

White Lake Area Chamber of Commerce
124 W. Hanson
Whitehall MI 49461-1027
(616) 893-4585

Whitmore Lake Chamber of Commerce
Box 454
Whitmore Lake MI 48189
(313) 449-8540

Williamston Area Chamber of Commerce   (517) 655-1549
Box 53
Williamston MI 48895

Wyoming Chamber of Commerce   (616) 531-5990
395 54th St. S.W.
Wyoming MI 49548-5614

Ypsilanti Convention and Visitors Bureau   (313) 482-4920
125 N. Huron St.
Ypsilanti MI 48197

Zeeland Chamber of Commerce   (616) 772-2494
9 S. Church St.
Zeeland MI 49464

Index

Acme: Amon Orchards and Grandma's Country Market, 177
Adrian: Lenawee County Historical Museum, 67; Siena Heights College, 119; Marvin's Fairfield Orchard, 174
Alamo Township, Kalamazoo County: Mildred Harris Sanctuary, 20; Alamo Township Museum, 79
Albion: Brueckner Museum and Gladsome Cottage Museum, 78; Gardner House Museum, 79; Albion College, 125; Harrison Orchard and Cider Mill, 175
Allen Park: Allen Park Symphony Orchestra, 103; Uniroyal Tire, 173
Allendale: Grand Valley State University, 128
Alma: Alma College, 131
Almena Township, Van Buren County: Martha Mott Preserve, 20
Alpena: Jesse Besser Museum, 88, 203; Alpena Community College, 133; Cripps Fruit Farm and Market, 176
Ann Arbor: Kelsey Museum of Archaeology, 73; Stearns Collection of Musical Instruments, 73; University of Michigan Museum of Art, 73; Ann Arbor Symphony Orchestra, 102; People Dancing, 102; Concordia College, 120; University of Michigan, 121; Washtenaw Community College, 122; Ann Arbor Art Fairs, 193
Armada: Blake's Orchard and Cider Mill, 174; Coon Creek Orchard and Cider Mill, 174
AuGres: Arenac County Historical Museum, 89
Au Train: Log Cabin Day, 189

Bad Axe: Pioneer Log Village, 90
Baraga: Copper Country State Forest, 50

Battle Creek: Art Center of Battle Creek, 78; Walking Tours, 154
Bay City: Nayanquing Point Wildlife Area, 54; Historical Museum of Bay County, 81; Bay City Players, 104; West Side, 156; Fireworks Festival, 197–98
Beaver Island: Beaver Head Light, 182
Bellaire: Bellaire Area Historical Museum, 91–92
Bellevue: Bellevue Memorial Museum, 81
Benton Harbor: Sarett Nature Center, 37; Lake Michigan College, 125; Log Cabin Day, 188; Blossomtime Festival, 194–95
Benzonia: Gwen Frostic Prints, 144
Berrien Springs: Siegfried H. Horn Archaeological Museum, 77; Lemon Creek Winery, 111, 115–16
Bessemer: Pumpkin Festival, 199
Bessemer Township, Gogebic County: Log Cabin Day, 189
Beulah: Platte River State Fish Hatchery, 58
Big Rapids: Ferris State University, 132, 209; Festival of the Arts, 197
Birmingham: Birmingham Bloomfield Art Association, 69; Birmingham-Bloomfield Symphony Orchestra, 102
Bloomfield Hills: E. L. Johnson Nature Center, 34–35
Bridgeport: Historical Society of Bridgeport, 87
Bridgman: Indiana Michigan Power Co. Cook Energy Information Center, 140–41
Brighton: Gage House, 86
Brimley: Hiawatha Forest National Fish Hatchery, 59; Pendills Creek National Fish Hatchery, 59; Point Iroquois Light Station, 96, 183
Brooklyn: Walker Tavern Historic Complex, 67

Buchanan: Madron Lake Hills Winery, 111; Tabor Hill Winery, 111
Burt Township, Cheboygan County: Colonial Point Forest Preserve, 21
Burton: For-Mar Nature Preserve and Arboretum, 38

Cadillac: Manistee National Forest, 16; Huron-Manistee National Forests, 42–44; MacKenzie Ski Trails, 47–48; Pere Marquette State Forest, 50; Johnson Hunting and Fishing Center, 95; Cadillac Area Symphony Orchestra, 106
Calumet: Walking Tour, 158
Canton: Canton Township Historical Museum, 74
Cassopolis: Pioneer Log Cabin Museum, 79; Log Cabin Day, 188
Cedar Springs: Red Flannel Festival, 195–96
Centreville: Glen Oaks Community College, 129
Charlotte: Conklin's Cider Mill, 176; Country Mill, 176
Cheboygan: Cheboygan Opera House, 105; Coast Guard Cutter *Mackinaw*, 149
Chelsea: Chelsea Milling Co., 139; Home-Town Heritage, 153; Chelsea Countryside, 162
Clawson: Clawson Historical Museum, 70
Clio: Ligon Outdoor Center, 39
Clyde Township, Allegan County: Fennville Farm, 18–19, 54
Colon: Leidy Lake State Game Area, 54
Concord: Mann House, 66
Convis Township, Calhoun County: Baker Sanctuary, 19
Covert Township, Van Buren County: Ross Preserve, 20

Davisburg: Davisburg Candle Factory, 139
Dearborn: Henry Ford Community College, 122; University of Michigan–Dearborn, 123–24
Detroit: Anna Scripps Whitcomb Conservatory, 35–36; Belle Isle Nature Center, 37; Belle Isle, 51; Children's Museum of the Detroit Public Schools, 74, 75; Moross House, 74; Dossin Great Lakes Museum, 75–76; Museum of African American History, 76; Pewabic Pottery, 76; Mme. Cadillac Dance Theatre, 103; Marygrove College, 123; University of Detroit Mercy, 123, 124; Wayne State University, 124–25; Detroit & Mackinac Brewery Ltd., 139, 140; Detroit Mounted Police, 147–48; Detroit Wastewater Treatment Plant, 148; U.S. District Court, 148; Elmwood Cemetery, 165; Belle Isle Aquarium, 172, 177–79; International Freedom Festival, 194; Miller Lite Montreux Detroit Jazz Festival, 193, 194
Dexter: Lakeview Farm and Cider Mill, 175
Douglas Township, Montcalm County: Comden-Towle Model Forest, 21
Dover Township, Otsego County: Hoobler Preserve, 21–22
Dowagiac: Southwestern Michigan College, 126
Drayton Plains: Drayton Plains Nature Center, 34
Drummond Island: Drummond Island Historical Museum, 96
Dryden Township, Lapeer County: Jonathon Woods Preserve, 17–18
Dundee: Old Mill Museum, 69
Durand: Michigan Railroad History Museum, 88

East Jordan: East Jordan Portside Art and Historical Museum, 92
East Lansing: Kresge Art Museum, 83, 84; Michigan State University Museum, 84; Michigan State University, 117, 131; Ag Expo, 197
Eaton Rapids: Veterans of Foreign Wars National Home, 184
Egelston Township, Muskegon County: Five Lakes Muskegon Nature Sanctuary, 24, 25–27
Elberta: Elberta Pier, 60
Elk Rapids: Elk Rapids Museum, 91; Walking Tour, 157
Elkton: Log Cabin Day, 188
Elmira: Jordan River National Fish Hatchery, 58
Empire: Sleeping Bear Dunes National Lakeshore, 5–7, 51
Erie Township, Monroe County: Erie Marsh Preserve, 18
Escanaba: Hiawatha National Forest, 44;

INDEX

Delta County Historical Museum, 97; William Bonifas Fine Arts Center, 97; Bay de Noc Community College, 135
Evart: Evart Public Library and Museum, 95
Eveline Township, Charlevoix County: Sleepy Hollow Nature Preserve, 23

Fallasburg: Fallasburg Covered Bridge, 180
Fennville: Fenn Valley Vineyards, 110–11
Flat Rock: Mazda Motor Manufacturing, 140
Flint: Chester H. Wilson Geology Museum, 82; Flint Youth Symphony Orchestra, 104; Flint Symphony Orchestra, 104; GMI Engineering and Management Institute, 130; Mott Community College, 130; University of Michigan–Flint, 130; Mott Lake Hostel, 207
Forest Home Township, Antrim County: Grass River Natural Area, 22
Frankenmuth: Bronner's Christmas Wonderland, 141–42, 143; Frankenmuth Flour Mill and General Store, 142–43; Frankenmuth Woolen Mill, 143–44; Zeilinger Wool Co., 144, 145
Frankfort: Frankfort Pier, 60; Brookwood Home Hostel, 207
Fremont: Gerber Products Co., 146; National Baby Food Festival, 198

Gaylord: Gaylord Area Wildlife Viewing Area, 49; Mackinaw State Forest, 50
Gladstone: Escanaba River State Forest, 50; Hoegh Pet Casket Co., 146
Gladwin: Log Cabin Day, 188
Glen Haven: Sleeping Bear Point Coast Guard Station, 93
Goodrich: Porter's Orchard, Farm Market and Cider Mill, 176
Grand Blanc: Grand Blanc Heritage Museum, 82
Grand Haven: U.S. Coast Guard Festival, 196–97
Grand Ledge: Museum of the Grand Ledge Area Historical Society, 81; Historic District, 156, 158–61
Grand Marais: Pictured Rocks National Lakeshore, 10–15; Lake Superior Forest Campground, 49; Grand Marais Maritime Museum, 95–96; Au Sable Point Light, 182, 183
Grand Rapids: Blandford Nature Center, 37; Kent Philharmonia Orchestra, 103; Le Montueux Vineyard and Winery, 112; Aquinas College, 127; Calvin College, 127; Grand Rapids Community College, 128; Kendall College of Art and Design, 128; Walking Tours, 155; Bin-An-Oan Orchards, 175; Robinette's Apple Haus and Gift Barn, 175; Log Cabin Day, 188
Grant Township, Keweenaw County: Estivant Pines Sanctuary, 25
Grayling: Au Sable River Canoe Marathon, 182
Greenleaf Township, Sanilac County: Sanilac Petroglyphs State Park, 184
Greenville: Klackle Orchards, 176; Wabasis Lake North Country Hostel, 207
Grosse Ile: Grosse Ile Historical Society, 76

Hamilton Township, Van Buren County: Hamilton Township Coastal Plain Marsh Nature Sanctuary, 20
Hancock: Finnish-American Heritage Center, 98; Houghton-Hancock Bridge, 180
Harbor Beach: Frank Murphy Museum, 89
Harbor Island National Wildlife Refuge, 30
Harbor Springs: West Wequetonsing Nature Preserve, 23–24
Harrietta: Harrietta State Fish Hatchery, 57, 58
Harrison: Mid Michigan Community College, 134
Harrisville: Harrisville Harbor, 60
Hastings: Cotant's Farm Market, 175
Hayes Township, Charlevoix County: Charles A. Ranson Nature Preserve, 23
Hiawatha Township, Schoolcraft County: Riverbank Sanctuary, 25
Hillsdale: Hillsdale College, 117–18
Holland: De Graaf Nature Center, 38; Holland Area Arts Council, 80; Hope College, 129; DeKlomp Wooden Shoe and Delftware Factory and Valdheer Tulip Gardens, 141, 142; Walking Tours, 155; Log Cabin Day, 188; Tulip Time Festival, 195, 196, 200–220
Holly: Diehl's Orchard and Cider Mill, 174
Homer: Blair Historical Farm, 78

Honor: Lake Township Park, 60
Houghton: Michigan Technological University, 136; Houghton-Hancock Bridge, 180
Houghton Lake: Houghton Lake Area Historical Society Village, 91
Howell: Howell Nature Center, 39–40
Hudson: Hudson Museum, 66–67
Huron Islands National Wildlife Refuge, 30

Imlay City: Imlay City Historical Museum, 66
Indian River: Cross in the Woods, 185
Interlochen: Walter E. Hastings Museum, 92; Interlochen Arts Camp, 105–6
Ironwood: Ottawa National Forest, 45–46; Old Depot Park Museum, 97; Hiawatha, 173
Isle Royale: Isle Royale National Park, 8–9
Ithaca: Gratiot County Area Historical Museum, 82

Jackson: Dahlem Environmental Education Center, 33; Civil War Muster, 192
Jordan Township, Antrim County: Jordan River, 22

Kalamazoo: Kalamazoo Institute of Arts, 80; Kalamazoo Symphony Orchestra, 103; Peterson & Sons Winery, 112; Kalamazoo Valley Community College, 126; Western Michigan University, 126–27; Historic District, 155
Kalkaska: Kalkaska County Historical Museum, 93
Kent City: Howard Christensen Nature Center, 38
Koehler Township, Cheboygan County: Agnes Andrae Nature Preserve, 21
Krakow Township, Presque Isle County: Thompson's Harbor, 22

Lake City: Log Cabin Day, 189
Lake Leelanau: Good Harbor Vineyards, 114
L'Anse: Bishop Baraga Shrine, 185, 186
Lansing: Carl G. Fenner Arboretum, 39; Telephone Pioneer Museum, 83; Michigan Historical Museum, 83; Boarshead: Michigan Public Theater, 104; Greater Lansing Symphony Orchestra, 104; State Capitol, 148–51; Peaks and Towers, 156; Mt. Hope Cemetery, 166
Lapeer: Apple Barn Cider Mill, 174
Lee Township, Calhoun County: Voorhees Sanctuary, 19
Leland: South Manitou Light, 182
Leoni Township, Jackson County: Haehnle Sanctuary, 17
Lincoln Township, Newaygo County: Loda Lake Wild Flower Sanctuary, 24
Little Traverse Township, Emmet County: Menonaqua Woods Nature Preserve, 23; Round Lake Nature Preserve, 23
Livonia: Livonia Youth Philharmonic, 103; Madonna University, 122; Schoolcraft College, 123

McMillan Township, Luce County: Sleeper Lake Sanctuary, 25
Mackinac Island: Tour, 164; U.S. Post Cemetery, 166–68
Mackinaw City: Mackinac Bridge Museum, 89; Mackinac Bridge Walk, 181, 189–91; Ironworkers International Festival, 198
Manchester: Sharon Mills Winery, 109–10
Manchester Township, Washtenaw County: Sharon Hollow Preserve, 18–19
Manistee: Lake Bluff Audubon Center, 41; Walking Tour, 157; Manistee National Forest Festival, 199
Manistique: Thompson State Fish Hatchery, 59; Schoolcraft County Historical Society, 98; Siphon Bridge, 180
Marcellus: Spirit Springs Farm, 175
Marine City: Pride and Heritage Museum, 72
Marquette: Marquette State Fish Hatchery, 59; Northern Michigan University, 136, 137; Northstar Home Hostel, 208
Marshall: Walking Tour, 154; Oakridge Cemetery, 166
Mattawan: Wolf Lake State Fish Hatchery, 57
Menominee: Log Cabin Day, 189
Midland: Chippewa Nature Center, 40; Automotive Hall of Fame, 86; Midland Art Council, 86; Midland County Historical Society, 86; Northwood Institute, 209

INDEX 245

Milford: Milford Historical Museum, 70; Heavner Home Hostel, 207
Millersburg: Hammond Bay Biological Station, 40
Mio: Au Sable State Forest, 50; Our Lady of the Woods Shrine, 185
Monroe: Monroe County Historical Museum, 68–69; River Raisin Battlefield Visitor Center, 69; Monroe County Community College, 119; Traces of Gen. George A. Custer, 152
Montague: Montague Museum, 94
Mt. Clemens: Michigan Transit Museum, 68; Selfridge Military Air Museum, 68
Mt. Pleasant: Center for Cultural and Natural History, 85; University Art Gallery, 85; Central Michigan University, 132
Mottville: Mottville Camelback Bridge, 180
Munger: Potato Festival, 197
Munising: Pictured Rocks National Lakeshore, 10–15; Twin Waterfalls Nature Preserve, 24; Munising Pier, 61
Muskegon: Muskegon County Museum, 94; Muskegon Museum of Art, 94; Muskegon Community College, 135; Heritage Village, 157

Negaunee: Iron Industry Museum, 98, 99–100
New Boston: Davies Orchard and Cider Mill, 175; Country Grandma's Home Hostel, 207
New Hudson: Serpent's Tooth Theatre, 102
Newberry: Lake Superior State Forest, 50
Newport: Detroit Edison Fermi 2 Power Plant, 138

Oden: Oden State Fish Hatchery, 58
Omena: Leelanau Wine Cellars, 114–15
Ontonagon: Ontonagon Light, 183
Oscoda: Au Sable River Canoe Marathon, 182
Oxford: Northeast Oakland Historical Museum, 70–71

Parisville: Log Cabin Day, 189
Paw Paw: St. Julian Wine Co., 112; Warner Vineyards, 113
Pearl Beach: Log Cabin Day, 188

Petoskey: North Central Michigan College, 134, 210
Pigeon: Pigeon Historical Depot Museum, 90
Plymouth: Plymouth International Ice Sculpture Spectacular, 194
Pokagon Township, Cass County: Dowagiac Woods, 20
Pontiac: Creative Arts Center, 71
Port Austin: Port Austin Pier, 60
Port Hope: Lighthouse Park Museum, 90
Port Huron: Waterworks Park, 60; Knowlton's Ice Museum, 71; Museum of Arts and History, 72; Coast Guard Cutter *Bramble*, 147; River Walks, 153; Blue Water Bridge, 180; Log Cabin Day, 188
Presque Isle Township, Presque Isle County: Besser Natural Area, 22

Raber Township, Chippewa County: Roach Point Nature Sanctuary, 24
Readmond Township, Emmet County: Elmer Johnson Nature Preserve, 23
Rochester: Dinosaur Hill Nature Preserve, 34; Yates Cider Mill, 174
Rochester Hills: Michigan Christian College, 120
Rogers City: Presque Isle County Historical Museum, 90; Nautical City Festival, 198
Romeo: Romeo Historical Museum, 68; Stony Creek Orchard and Cider Mill, 174; Verellen Orchards and Cider Mill, 174
Roscommon: Kirtland Community College, 133
Rutland Township, Barry County: Warner Sanctuary, 21

Saginaw: Shiawassee National Wildlife Refuge, 30–32; Saginaw Art Museum, 87; Saginaw Railway Museum, 88; Saginaw Symphony Orchestra, 105; Saginaw Symphony Youth Orchestra, 105; Bintz Apple Farm and Cider Mill, 176
St. Charles: St. Charles Waterfowl Observatory, 54
St. Clair: St. Clair Historic Museum, 71
St. Ignace: Mackinac Bridge Walk, 181, 189–91
St. Johns: Beck's Cider Mill, 176; Uncle John's Cider Mill, 176; Mint Festival, 196–97

St. Joseph: Fort Miami Heritage Society, 77; Krasl Art Center, 77; SculpTur, 154; Blossomtime Festival, 194
Saline: Walking Tour, 153; Windy Ridge Orchard and Cider Mill, 175
Sault Ste. Marie: Lake Superior State University, 135; Pathway to Historic Churches, 158; Soo Locks, 171
Seney: Seney National Wildlife Refuge, 28–29, 31
Shelby: Shelby Gem Factory, 146
Shepherd: Shepherd Historical Society Museum and Little Red Schoolhouse Museum, 85
Sidney: Montcalm Community College, 132; Log Cabin Day, 188
Skanee: Second Sand Beach County Park, 61
South Haven: Liberty Hyde Bailey Museum, 80
Southfield: Actors Alliance Theatre Company, 101; Scandinavian Symphony, 102; Lawrence Technological University, 120
Spring Arbor: Spring Arbor College, 119
Spring Arbor Township, Jackson County: Kate Palmer Bird Sanctuary, 17
Springfield Township, Oakland County: Timberland Swamp Nature Preserve, 18
Sterling Heights: Sterling Heights Nature Center, 34
Stockbridge: Dewey School Museum, 66
Suttons Bay: L. Mawby Vineyards, 114

Tawas City: Tawas Point Light, 182
Thompson: Thompson Creek Mouth, 61
Traverse City: Schooner *Madeline*, 92; Chateau Grand Traverse, 114; Northwestern Michigan College, 134; Candle Factory, 145; Inland Seas Education Association, 184–85; National Cherry Festival, 198
Trenton: Elizabeth Park, 60; Trenton Historical Museum, 76
Troy: Lloyd A. Stage Outdoor Education Center, 35; Troy Museum and Historic Village, 71
Twin Lake: Owasippe Museum, 94

University Center: Marshall M. Fredericks Sculpture Gallery, 87; Delta College, 129; Saginaw Valley State University, 133

Vanderbilt: Pickerel Lake Forest Campground, 49
Vermontville: Vermontville Museum, 81

Waterford: Hess-Hathaway Park, 35; Oakland Youth Orchestra, 102
West Bloomfield: Holocaust Memorial Center, 70
White Cloud: North Country Trail Association, 208
Wyoming: Grace Bible College, 209

Ypsilanti: Eastern Michigan University, 121

www.ingramcontent.com/pod-product-compliance
Lightning Source LLC
Chambersburg PA
CBHW021139230426

43667CB00005B/187